IOU to Mr. Slatty

~~Peter Rakita 3~~

~~Aaron Rees 3~~

Cassidy Carroll 35

Caroline 3

Alissa 3

Jacob K 3.00

David S.

Evan Clurosinger 3.000

~~Paul Mayr 3~~

~~Hailey Heinberg $3~~

~~Mica Marty $3.00~~

Levi Poletti

~~Jackson~~ Sage $300

~~Linnea $3.00~~

Grant M. $3.00

Olivia T. $3.00

Nick M $3.00

~~Audrey W. $3.00~~

Pete 3.00

Joe — 1.00

20 Minutes to a Top Performer

Three *Fast* and Effective Conversations to MOTIVATE, DEVELOP, AND ENGAGE Your Employees

Alan Vengel

New York Chicago San Francisco Lisbon London
Madrid Mexico City Milan New Delhi San Juan
Seoul Singapore Sydney Toronto

The **McGraw·Hill** Companies

1 2 3 4 5 6 7 8 9 0   FGR/FGR   0 1 0 9

ISBN: 978-0-07-162931-7
MHID: 0-07-162931-9

McGraw-Hill books are available at special quantity discounts to use as premiums and sales promotions, or for use in corporate training programs. To contact a representative please e-mail us at bulksales@mcgraw-hill.com

This book is printed on acid-free paper.

For Kathleen and David

CONTENTS

Foreword

Now more than ever, we are forced to do more and more with less and less. We expect more from our employees with less training, more results with less time, more profits with less investment, and even more customer service with less effort on the part of (naturally) fewer employees!

The economic downturn has only made things more difficult for the increasingly burdened manager. So I was pleased to see that my colleague and long-time friend, Alan Vengel, has worked his magic in this new book. Why are these 20-Minute Conversations that Alan writes about in his book so important all the time? Why are they important in an up economy—and doubly vital during a down economy? The times are indeed changing, and with change comes progress—and with progress comes more work, harder work, and increasing pressures for the continually put-upon manager.

I remember when organizations had the luxury of being able to hire professional managers, managers who managed as their full-time—and only—job. Today we have what I call managers-plus: managers-plus-recruiters, managers-plus–production specialists, managers-plus-cheerleaders, managers-plus-creative, managers-plus-plus!

This supersize, value-plus style of management isn't going away anytime soon. If you find yourself uncomfortable in the role of manager-plus-counselor-plus-coach-plus-motivator-plus-mentor, these ideas should make the part you're most uncomfortable with comfortable so that you don't avoid it.

Alan's ideas enable today's busy managers to do something they haven't done in quite some time: relax. The minute they hear "20 minutes," managers start to relax; the minute they hear "five-minute prep," they start to relax even more. The more that managers can be provided with the tips, the tools, and the how-to's, the easier it will be for them to have these conversations along with everything else they have on their plate.

The best part is, these conversations aren't rocket science; they're what you do every day anyway, just with a little more guided focus. The importance of these conversations isn't so much in your technique or the setting or, occasionally, even the content; what really matters to your people is the conversation itself.

In my own research on retention and engagement, I continue to learn that it's the conversation itself that makes people feel valued, needed, and appreciated. It can be as simple as a manager stopping for literally minutes to say, "Here's what I appreciate; here's what you did well," even to those people we think already know how they're doing. Quite often, they really don't know how they're doing; just as often, your assumed lack of feedback can leave them stranded, thinking that they're doing far worse than they actually are—or far better. My research and that of my colleagues points over and over again to the fact that people don't leave organizations; they leave bad managers. What makes a bad manager? The manager who doesn't nurture, appreciate, coach, motivate, or mentor his or her people.

Alan's book helps you do all of the above—and then some.

Now, many managers who scan this book will probably think that they have heard all of this before. You know that your people need feedback. You know that you should be communicating with them more. You know that they need to be motivated and even mentored from time to time. You know this stuff but . . . have you done it lately? And if so, how lately? Last week, last month . . . or last year?

If it hasn't been in the last week or two, read on.

Workers of all ages want to learn; they understand that not all career paths lead to upward mobility, but they want to know that their careers offer other rewards, such as personal creativity, ownership of ideas, and the chance to be rewarded emotionally, professionally, and even creatively from time to time. If you're not holding frequent career conversations, you are probably making assumptions about what your employees really want.

In this economy, it's critical to let people know how valued they are; *20 Minutes to a Top Performer* will teach you how to let your people know that you value them, creatively and constructively, emotionally and effectively.

The beauty of Alan's ideas is that they don't require a lot of fancy technology, new equipment, or high-tech gadgetry. There is no task force to create, no commission to deputize, no proprietary license to buy and download; in fact, you don't even need a computer, PDA, stylus, or Internet connection. You already have what is required: two ears and one mouth—and in just that order.

Alan reintroduces us to the long-forgotten art of conversation. Not the "jump-in-the-moment-the-other-person-finishes" method, but truly the art of listening more than we speak and making what we say that much more powerful in the bargain.

His book shows us that beyond making people feel good, 20-Minute Conversations are just plain good business. Problems are solved in a proven, practical, and effective way, to the mutual benefit of both the manager and the employee. Alan introduces a model of cooperative collaboration that requires that elusive quality that most companies offer but never really deliver: true ownership.

—Beverly Kaye, October 2009

ACKNOWLEDGMENTS

My work on this book has really been the effort of many.

First, I would like to thank my clients and all the workshop participants who have allowed me the freedom to perfect behavior models and gather new research.

And, I want to thank Carol Green-Lloyd, Tony Lloyd, Russell Fischer, Robert Diforio, Beverly Kaye, Devon Scheef, Karen Farmer, Ellen McGinnis, Yolanda Perusse, and all the team at Career Systems International for their support, advice, editing and suggestions throughout the project.

And of course, my appreciation to the great professionals at McGraw-Hill Publishers, Mary Glenn, Knox Huston, Daina Penikas and all the others who have helped make this work a joyful and fun experience!

INTRODUCTION:
WHY 20 MINUTES?

What can change the direction of history, the course of a life, the value of a relationship, or the tone and tenor of the day-to-day workplace? What can influence decisions, foster respect, generate passion, motivate employees, and create a true team rather than a collective "I"? What can create top performers out of mere performers?

What can help you influence others and manage and lead more effectively?

Words.

Conversations.

Conversations bridge the gap between people who have different values, different views, and different backgrounds. A conversation can speak volumes or cover up dirty little secrets. Conversations can unite or divide a workplace. A conversation can bridge party politics, mend opposing views, and bring people together.

Conversations give voice to your leadership. Every day, in every way, whether you are speaking one-on-one or inspiring the troops, your words have weight, value, and meaning. Words send signals—sometimes smoke signals, sometimes alarm bells. A hundred conversations a week tell people what your priorities are, how you value others, what's on your mind, and *who you are as a leader.*

Conversations at work and outside of work aren't so different.

Most of us wonder, "What do I say? How do I begin? How can I keep the conversational ball rolling? How can I candidly say what I need to and still keep the relationship intact?" Conversation is defined as a "daily expression and exchange of individual opinions."

For the uninitiated, there are two types of conversations:

1. *Disruptive conversations.* A bad conversation is "disruptive"; it sets you apart from others, rather than drawing them in. People know when they're in a disruptive conversation; its earmarks are platitudes, false niceties, passive-aggressiveness, and the almost total absence of true listening. When you speak *to* others rather than speaking *with* them, you are engaging in disruptive conversations.

2. *Connective conversations.* A good conversation is "connective"; it invites people to participate. It's not a lecture. It's not a harangue. A connective conversation is two people equally exchanging their views and perceptions, reserving judgment, and applying logic. All connective conversations have some common characteristics. They're truthful. They build trust and relationship. They come from positive motives.

Conversations are not absolutes; on any given day, we can flip-flop from disruptive to connective conversations, and flip right back again. Nor are conversations one-sided. As Charles Schwab once said, "It's not a conversation if only one person is talking."

The purpose of this book is *not* to tell you how wrong you are when your speaking is disruptive. The purpose of this book is to *help* you see the value of conversations—quick, efficient conversations—in crafting top performers in your organization and to help you find and fine-tune your leadership voice so that your conversations are connective, powerful, and positive and get results.

There is never enough time to do everything, but there is always enough time to do the most important thing.

—Brian Tracy

Results Speak Louder than Words

Most managers would agree that somewhere in their charter, getting results plays a vital role in achieving personal and professional success. And for many managers, achieving technical or project results comes naturally. But the key to long-term organizational and leadership success is *moving employees to action*.

Never before in the history of the modern workforce have organizations and the managers in them been more in need of talented, committed people. Managers realize that the daily leadership of their employees is critical, yet many of them do not know how to help the people who work for them make significant changes in how they do their work.

Communication is key. Communicating what you want your employees to do and actually getting them to do it creates one of the largest gulfs between managers and employees in any organization. To bridge that gulf, effective leaders know how to have three distinct types of conversations with their employees:

- *Conversations that change performance.* First, effective leaders know when and how to use coaching. They recognize both the value and the effectiveness of being successful coaches in an environment based on teamwork. Coaching moves people to action by focusing on *performance* and *feedback*.

- *Conversations that keep people interested in and satisfied with their work.* Second, effective leaders are comfortable with motivating. Great leaders know that they do not need to be mind readers and that they need to be able to involve others to "translate" thoughts and ideas into words and actions that encourage employees. Motivating moves people to action by focusing on *engagement* and *interests*.

- *Conversations that keep people learning and ready for the future.* Third, these managers are savvy mentors. Not only do they find mentors for themselves, but they offer mentorship to those in need. This can take the form of giving advice or imparting verbal wisdom, but, just as often, it can mean leading by responsible example. Mentoring moves people to action by focusing on *supporting* and *developing*.

This book, *20 Minutes to a Top Performer: Three Fast and Effective Conversations to Motivate, Develop, and Engage Your Employees*, dissects these three important conversations and explains *how*, *why*, and, just as importantly, *when* each conversation is appropriate for a particular situation.

Over the last 25 years, I have presented seminars, programs, and keynotes to more than 500 corporations as a consultant and speaker. For the last 5 years, I have been handing out a questionnaire to all the participants in my training classes—culminating in responses from more than 4,300 managers and employees. The most important question being answered boiled down to, "Who are the most effective leaders you have had, and what did they do that made them effective?" The answer to this question, along with other research, has formed the basis of the approach in this book.

Based on these responses, we have developed a new mindset for leaders that helps to reduce stress for both leaders and employees. As a result of this research, leaders have enjoyed a more direct, clean, and concise way to communicate, and employees have stopped wondering what their managers really want.

We now have a direction and purpose for each conversation, avoiding the tendency to mix these conversations up and thus create unnecessary confusion in the mind of an employee concerning what these conversations are about. And leaders are no longer frustrated by having to use time for these conversations, but getting vague results because their approaches have been vague to begin with. Consequently, leaders can have shorter, more impactful conversations, and employees can produce faster results because they now know exactly what is expected of them.

Hence, *20 Minutes to a Top Performer*.

Conversation: The Voice of Leadership— 20-Minute Conversations That Get Results

The good news is that managers already know how to use most of the skills involved in *coaching*, *motivating*, and *mentoring* top performers. For many of us, we simply need to hone these skills so that we are more purposeful and efficient, and also figure out when best to use them. I believe that you will find this book realistic and useful. It's been especially designed to be interactive and practical for busy managers with many responsibilities and too little time for people management.

Great leaders grow great people. And a key to that growth is a leader's ability to move people to action through performance and development conversations. In today's fast-paced, ever-changing, overstressed work environment, these conversations need to be not just *effective*, but also meaningful.

In their book *The Value Imperative: Managing for Superior Shareholder Returns* (Free Press, 1994), management experts

James McTaggart, Peter Kontes, and Michael Mankins contend that "Leaders come out of meetings without clear decisions." Your people need to walk away and think that the time was well spent.

The day-to-day pace of business leaves most managers with little time and energy for developing the people who report to them. "Leaders—spend too much time meeting," conclude the authors of *The Value Imperative*, "when they have no clear agendas—and are unfocused as to specific outcomes."

By developing their ability to have focused, outcome-oriented conversations that engage and motivate their talented people, any manager can be a successful developer of top performers.

Overall, *20 Minutes to a Top Performer* will help you develop your ability to get excellent results by

- Learning about three critical leadership conversations—*coaching, motivating,* and *mentoring*—and when and how to have them
- Examples of real business leadership behaviors that move people to action
- How to build 20-Minute Conversations for immediate application

The gift of gab truly is given to most of us at birth; we are born instinctively knowing how—and when—to get what we want. Truly, anyone can twist things around to get his or her way once. To truly succeed in business, however, you have to achieve your goals again and again, often with the same people.

That takes honest influence skills, the kind that allow you to look the other person in the eye, even as you push for what you want. It's not just a win/win but a win/win/win situation because it's right for *you*, for *the business*, and for *the employee*.

You'll find that *20 Minutes to a Top Performer* is not a book full of complicated models or tricks; it offers sound wisdom and sage advice on quick, efficient, time-sensitive dialogue for the extremely busy leader in all of us. That's it: 20-Minute Leadership Conversations. No more; no less.

But it's just what you need to succeed.

Less Really *Is* More

What if I told you that, in 20 minutes or less, you could influence your employees to be more successful, enjoy their work more, and play as a team more effectively than through any 60- or 120-minute knock-down, drag-out confrontational sit-down?

What if I added that in addition to getting more, faster, and better results from your employees, you too could gain important feedback and critical direction from your own employers in just 20 minutes or less?

You can, you know, merely by putting *20 Minutes to a Top Performer* into practice.

Coaching moves people to action by focusing on performance and feedback. So forget coaching that is a drawn out complicated dialogue. This is *next-generation coaching*, coaching the way it needs to be. And this is coaching with a time limit: a 20-Minute Conversation that changes the results you get as a leader and builds and maintains your employees' success with the work they do.

We've all mourned at the mass grave of "death by committee." We've all endured countless, endless, interminable meetings, conference calls, and meet and greets where little gets accomplished, but much time is wasted; *20 Minutes to a Top Performer* is the antidote to that grim corporate reality. As a result, you get what you, the business, and your employees all want: *more results in less time*.

Why 20 Minutes?

Why put a time limit on leadership? Simple: research suggests that not only can human beings *not concentrate for long periods of time*, but they can typically concentrate on *only one thing at a time*. Clearly, leaders who lack focus and direction and who spend too long meandering through yet another hour-long meeting with no agenda—and very little audience retention— will fall behind rather than surge ahead.

Case in point: a study by the University of Chicago Business School professors found that "leaders need to be efficient in their communications, while setting clear high standards—and persistent in what they need from others."

It's a little like exercise; I read once that with anything over 75 minutes in one workout, you're really doing more harm than good. So why work out for 90 minutes when 60 minutes is actually *more* effective? Likewise, adult learning theory tells us that people can take in only about 10 minutes of continuous input, after which they stop absorbing much information. Clearly, meetings need to be shorter, not longer—but no less effective no matter despite how long or short they may be.

Time is not the only issue that promises to make 20-Minute Leadership Conversations a vital part of your leadership style. A University of Iowa study offers convincing evidence that adults can focus on only one thing at a time, stating, "We must focus the learning. Be successful with one issue at a time in conversations of 15–20 minute duration."

This theme was reinforced in *The Owner's Manual for the Brain* by researchers and authors Geoffrey Woodman and Steven Luck, who state, "Adults can only learn one new skill at a time—pay attention to it—focus without distractions."

The goal of using conversations with both time limits *and* a clear goal is not to spend all your time coaching—or even motivating or mentoring—top performers in your organization. The goal is to lead every time, with efficient time. In fact, 20-Minute Leadership Conversations are merely tools toward that end, not the end itself. When you've mastered the structure of these conversations, you will actually think about them less and do them more. As a result, your leadership will be more focused, efficient, and productive; mere performers will become top performers.

So why, specifically, *20 Minutes to a Top Performer?*

- Because you don't have time, and you need to get results

- Because you are continuously being asked to do more with less
- Because ultimately the leader is responsible, so your career is on the line
- Because no one ever told you everything that you could do in a structured 20-Minute Conversation
- Because you don't need another long drawn-out meeting
- Because your employees desperately need these 20 minutes with you
- Because leaders need to be purposeful, clean, and quick in how they communicate
- Because you need to take care of yourself first and need a purposeful 20 minutes with your boss
- And did I already mention that you don't have time, but you need results?

Now more than ever, time is of the essence. Do you even have time to read this book? Of course not! That's why I've made this book quick, simple, and usable immediately, so that everyone, regardless of education, background, or position, can create organizational rock stars with *20 Minutes to a Top Performer*.

Arnold Palmer used to talk about "charging the course." What he meant by that was having an "approach with a purpose." So this book is about purpose, speed, and results; it's not about long discussions or management philosophies. It's about having clear goals for your conversation and getting clear decisions and specific results from your team.

When Is the 20-Minute Conversation Useful?

The 20-Minute Leadership method can be used for many different leadership conversations, but we will begin with a focus on three key conversations that every leader needs to have:

1. Coaching for performance
2. Motivating for engagement
3. Mentoring for development

In my research, I have found that these three conversations make up the foundation for leading people to action. I've been a consultant to Fortune 1000 companies for more than 25 years, and over the last 5 years, I decided to undertake a study of what employees need most from their leaders and to answer the probing question, "What behaviors and characteristics do these leaders exhibit?" Throughout this book, we will look at and explore the research I've compiled along with the best practices from industry leaders on these subjects. What, exactly, will you discover throughout *20 Minutes to a Top Performer*?

In *Part 1* of this book, we will focus on the first of the three 20-Minute Leadership Conversations: coaching. Many people feel that they already know everything they need to know about coaching; this section clears up many misconceptions and clearly focuses not only on why coaching is different from motivating or mentoring, but in which cases you will find coaching to be the most effective conversation of the three.

In *Chapter 1* we will look at how to make the 20-Minute Coaching Conversation work, in practical, real-life terms.

First, we'll review best practices and research to determine the need for performance coaching, then we'll explore the value of Push and Pull behaviors, and finally we'll provide specific relief with the quick coaching five-minute plan called "positive preparation."

We'll also examine real coaching conversations from stories of leaders who have been challenged by time and different performance situations, like Beth, a new manager who inherits a team of talented performers who are underperforming as if they were enjoying their mediocrity. And Sharon, who has 10 things to correct with her direct report, but does not know where to start, how to focus on specifics or how to find the time.

In each chapter, I will also include specific tips, strategies, and exercises that you can *try now*. These are things that you can do immediately to make a difference in how you influence for results quickly.

Chapters 2 and 3 challenge our preconceived notions about feedback; and we all have them. In *Chapter 2* we'll talk about the pros and cons of feedback and why it is so vitally important that you do it right. In *Chapter 3* we'll narrow the focus slightly to how, exactly, to give valuable rather than negligible feedback and help create top performers through this simple mechanism. Along the way, we'll meet folks like Eric, a VP of finance at a large high-tech company who said that his sixth-grade teacher never rewarded him for failing less—and how learning to give feedback helped him profit from his teacher's mistake.

In *Part 2* we will take the mystery out of motivation; we will look at how motivation engages and retains the key talent you need if you are to succeed. You'll be introduced to folks like Robert, who on his first day of work hears from his coworker Bill, "Don't count on any support from your manager; they don't come with any backbone at all!" And we'll learn how effective leaders can keep both current employees and new hires motivated from day one.

Chapter 4 explores how to first keep yourself fully engaged, because you need to be at your best if you are to motivate and engage your people. We will also introduce a "motivational engagement" survey that allows you to assess what keeps you interested in and excited about your work. Intrinsic motivation includes things that you really have control over and can use with your team to keep people engaged and energetic.

There has been lots of research on what truly motivates people, and in *Chapter 5*, we will look at some of these things more closely. (Here's a spoiler: *it's not money!*) We'll keep it simple and usable, with sections like "Four Reasons Why Leaders Don't Ask" and "The Seven Behaviors of the 20-Minute Motivation Conversation." We'll also hear from leaders like Sarah, for whom her annual bonus was only part of her motivation; the other (perhaps bigger) part of her motivation and engagement in the project was the challenge and the acknowledgement of a job well done. We'll also meet Sarah's boss, Jeff, and a company VP, both of whom didn't quite get Sarah's motivation and, as a result, left one very disgruntled employee in their wake.

In *Chapter 6*, we'll look at easy exercises you can do that will allow you to reengage your people and hold 20-Minute

Conversations that are concrete, focused, and result in action leading to meaningful work. After reading "Six Essential Truths about Motivation and Engagement," you'll better understand why top performers require competent motivators.

Part 3 takes a look at the 20-Minute Mentoring Conversation by developing a key role for leaders: the mentor. People need many mentors, not just their bosses. But the boss does play an important part for an employee as a developer, guide, and advice giver.

Too many leaders give up this role over time—or never make an attempt to fulfill it in the first place. And many employees have an emptiness and a craving for this type of conversation. In just 20 minutes, you will be able to construct and hold this important conversation.

Chapter 7 helps you help your top performers by learning to start where they are, not where you are. This critical skill can help leaders mold top performers like Linda, who needs help with negotiating—and gets it when her leader sets her up with a negotiating mentor. Top performers need TLC, but the right kind of TLC; mentorship requires knowing what to say to the right person at the right time, and in *Chapter 8*, I reveal how storytelling can become a big part of that process.

Along the way, I will help you put this mentoring conversation together. We'll look in detail at why it's needed and how to keep it to the point, with clear goals and outcomes, so that both the leader and the employee have a sense of future possibilities and developmental opportunities.

In *Chapter 9*, you'll meet a potential top performer named Dale, who his boss feels has grown a little too comfortable in his position to live up to his full potential. You'll be able to see how, through proper mentoring, Dale's boss encourages him to become a top performer and how, ultimately, she puts the tools for success into his hands.

Chapter 10 combines everything you've learned so far and asks the critical, very realistic question, "What if nothing works?" Here you will discover the three typical forms of resistance and learn how to manage them effectively with my three-step response to resistance.

Finally, in the *Appendix*, I've included additional worksheets, tips for success, and strategies for development, including ideas on increasing your influence throughout the organization.

So if you're ready, your first 20 Minutes of Conversation await you.

Best is to know—and know you know.
Next best is to know that you don't know.
Third best is knowing, but not realizing it.
Worst is not to know that you don't know.

—Ancient Proverb

PART I

THE 20-MINUTE COACHING CONVERSATION

CHAPTER 1

COACHING THAT INVOLVES AND INITIATES ACTION

---

coach \ *kōch* \ <u>v.</u> to train intensively as by instruction and demonstration; <u>n.</u> one who instructs or trains a performer or team of performers; a private tutor

---

When leaders use the wrong tone of voice—a voice that's tentative and unclear—they give signals to everyone else, and, as a result, teams can get off course quickly. As these signals spread from top to bottom, suddenly it becomes okay for the rest of the team to be tentative and vague as well. It's easier for everybody; if no one knows what the stakes really are, then they can't really be all that high, and we can all relax.

Coaching is the opposite of vague; it's about clarity—for you, for the organization, and for your people. In his work writing about corporate courage in such books as *Right Risk* and *Courage Goes to Work*, author Bill Treasurer talks about a concept called "Jump First," which means that leaders need to set the standard when it comes to clarity. In other words, they need to be good role models for the kind of behavior they want their team to exhibit.

Unfortunately, this continues to be a companywide issue across the country. According to Lake Research Partners, a leading public opinion research firm, "Employees don't know where they stand on what their leaders think about their performance. The research also states that employees not only don't get the feedback to improve performance but 33 percent state they don't get the recognition for any success!"

If a leader is wishy-washy when it comes to feedback and recognition, his team will be wishy-washy about expectations and performance. If a leader is direct and to the point, providing both feedback *and* recognition, her team will come to see this as standard operating procedure and will rise to this level as well.

Author Ferdinand Fournies collected information on thousands of leaders and managers and concluded that there are several reasons why employees do not get the results they are looking for. The number one reason? Employees don't know what they are supposed to do! (And a close second: they don't know why they are supposed to do it!)

An October 2008 *Wall Street Journal* article cites research by the Hay Group detailing what leaders need to do to manage more effectively, especially if they tend to micromanage. These findings support the following three principles of quick, focused conversations that you will learn, practice, and master in *20 Minutes to a Top Performer*:

1. *State clear expectations.* This saves time and helps people know what success looks like.
2. *Encourage questions and suggestions.* This gets all parties involved in solutions.
3. *Offer constructive feedback.* This ensures that employees can hit the target.

So the tone of your 20-Minute Coaching Conversation must be clear and to the point; clarity should be first and foremost. The leader is demonstrating how coaching communication *should* be done—leading by example, so to speak. And in the work I have been doing, I have found that leaders *do* set the tone for the kind of communication that people have with one another. The entire team will pick up on the mindset of the leader.

You can see this research in real time simply by looking objectively at your own office. Is it hectic and frenzied, but competent and efficient? If so, chances are that's your own personal leadership style. Is it ordered and quiet? Loud and coarse? Rude and ambitious? Calm and calculated? The apple doesn't far fall from the tree, and it's important to see the strengths and weaknesses of the team as your own—and vice versa.

Managers really do have a lot of influence on their people, and they are always surprised by how closely they are watched for clues on how to act and behave. People will do as the leader does. Having productive 20-Minute Coaching Conversations sends a clear message to the team that we will be purposeful with our conversations and conscious of their effects.

Few activities are as damaging to pace and progress as unfulfilling conversations. Wasted words spend breath, time, and productivity with little or no return on investment; conscious, active, and clear conversations boost morale and productivity by sending a clearer signal to your people about deliverables and expectations.

Research indicates that not only is coaching becoming less effective, but it's taking longer and longer to produce less and less. In a study by BlessingWhite, a survey of 710 managers found that 33 percent felt that "coaching is too time-consuming." In a global survey, up to 42 percent of 2,000 managers around the world indicate that coaching is taking too long. Time is precious; 29 percent of leaders complain that they just have too many direct reports for time-intensive coaching.

I know what you're thinking: "With all that's on my plate, with as many employees as I have, now you're telling me to hit them up one-on-one for better results? Do you know how long that's going to take?"

I absolutely know how long it's going to take because I've been sharing my 20-Minute Leader philosophy with managers all over the country for years. What I've learned is that the less time you have the more effective you have to make every minute. Trust me, these 20 minutes could pay off in ways that include higher ROI, more effective employees, better sales—you name it.

More specifically, you don't have the time *not* to do it.

At the end of the day, we are all here to get work done. Creating a winning template for your own 20-Minute Coaching Conversations merely sends the message that you care about productivity to the point of being clear, concise, and compelling in your day-to-day interactions with staff and team members. In turn, they will act accordingly.

Managers who are more open and straightforward in their business dealings build credibility with their direct reports. When they have the courage to say what they need in a direct, no-nonsense manner, people know where they stand and what is expected of them. Again, the key word here is *clarity*. When the leader is a role model for clear, direct communication, the message to the rest of the team is that we can be clear and direct with one another.

Great minds have purposes, others have wishes.

—Washington Irving

Push Behaviors

Behaviors that help managers be clear and direct are what we call *Push behaviors*. In other words, they are behaviors that "push" against one another to achieve the desired result of clarity.

In our surveys while conducting research with more than 4,300 managers and employees over the last five years, my colleagues and I have found that more than 73 percent of respondents want two key things from their leaders at work:

1. More direction
2. Direction that is specific and to the point

People really want to know what others want from them, and one of the biggest complaints these respondents had was not knowing what their leaders wanted from them specifically. We have a behavior model that we use to help managers be more specific and direct, and it works around this Push energy. And it's not really as harsh as it sounds—it's really just being able to say exactly what you want.

For example, here are three Push behaviors:

1. *Asserting:* "I want . . ."; I would like . . ."; "I need . . ."; "You should do . . ."
2. *Suggesting:* "My recommendation is . . ."; "Here is my idea . . ."; "Let's try this . . ."; "Here is my suggestion . . ."
3. *Reasoning:* "I have two reasons for this . . ."; "Here is why this is important . . ."

The Consequences of Fearing the Push

Some leaders see Push behaviors as being too confrontational or aggressive, but at what price do they risk losing control of their team by not pushing just a little harder for control? For instance, look at this example of what happens when Push behaviors are not used appropriately or when managers are afraid to use Push behaviors because they might be seen as being too pushy.

Jim, an employee, enters his boss, Sharon's, office. "You wanted to see me, Sharon?" he asks.

Sharon replies, "Yes, Jim. I was wondering how the second stage of the project is coming along."

Jim replies a little hesitantly, "Okay, well, we have just the one analysis back from Ben's group, and we're refining the data now."

Sharon looks concerned but replies, "Oh, okay. Well, I guess that's fine. When will you be ready to show it to me and the other team leaders?"

Jim answers, "In about two weeks or so."

Sharon now seems slightly more alarmed. "So long?" she asks, getting a little emotional. "Not any sooner than that?"

Jim explains, "Well, it will take at least two weeks; one of my people is out on vacation."

Sharon sighs. "Well, okay. I just didn't realize it would take so long."

Jim leaves Sharon's office scratching his head and wondering what *that* was all about. Why was Sharon so upset about his estimated timeline? Did she need the results sooner? Didn't she know that one of his people was on vacation, and that this would delay the results? When she finally said, "I guess it's okay," Sharon didn't seem to really object to its taking two weeks. Despite the odd interaction, Jim leaves the meeting assuming that Sharon is okay with his deadline, and doesn't change anything about how he's getting her the results she wants.

For her part, Sharon leaves the meeting thinking, "I really wanted to show this material to my director by the beginning of next week, Tuesday at the latest. Now it's going to look like my team just can't create the work fast enough. Jim may not be the right person for this job; he just does not have a sense of urgency."

Who was right? Who was wrong? In the end, it's all about results, and this meeting created none of the above. What really happened is that Jim did not get the message about when Sharon needed the data; he hears only that she wanted to know when he would have the project done. If Sharon had *pushed* more specifically with Jim by saying something clear and specific like, "Jim, I really need those results sooner—next Tuesday afternoon by 3 p.m.," then the two of them could have problem-solved together by generating some ideas and actions that could meet Sharon's needs while giving Jim a specific deadline.

But now Jim is feeling a bit confused about what the meeting was *really* about in the first place. He's feeling as if maybe Sharon is checking up on him, questioning his timeline and maybe even his judgment—not a good place for a team leader to be in. And suddenly Sharon is having doubts about Jim's ability to do the work. Because she did not use appropriate behaviors, the meeting is misleading and unfair to both parties concerned.

As we can see, the factor that was missing from this confusing meeting was *clarity*. Push behaviors could have resolved the situation quickly and effectively without ill feelings on either side of the equation.

This is one way to facilitate a 20-Minute Coaching Conversation. Push behaviors cut through the clutter that tends to make otherwise short meetings long. Another aspect of facilitating a 20-Minute Coaching Conversation includes the element of something called Pull energy.

Get 'Em Talking by Using Pull Energy

A sales training expert I know once invited me to sit in on one of her sales seminars. After I had made a presentation to the group, trying out some of the key selling concepts, she gave me some quick, knee-jerk feedback: "Keep it simple, Stupid."

I understood immediately what she meant—I had overcomplicated my short presentation—but I also took slight offense at the "stupid" part of her feedback. It wasn't me she was calling stupid, of course; it was my presentation. Yet in the companies I go to and while working with the participants in my workshops, I have found that these people are far from stupid. In fact, they are some of the smartest people I know.

They know a lot, and, like me in my sales seminar presentation that day, they want to get it all out there. So, again like me, they talk too much about it. After all, they have a lot to say and a lot to share.

Far from being stupid, good leaders are sometimes too smart for their own good. (And yes, being "too smart" *can* be a bad thing.) Not only do they know what's wrong and needs to be fixed, but they want to fix it too quickly—and (usually) by themselves.

It is said, "May the best person for the job win." And quite often, the leader *is* the best person for the job. But of all the smart, competent, multitasking, self-starting leaders I've met over the years, there isn't one who can run a company single-handedly. So sometimes knowing the *next* best person for the job is actually being the best leader you can be.

If leaders identify coaching issues and then solve the issues on their own, they are taking ownership of the solutions—and most of the time this will leave out the employees' opportunity to contribute to the solution.

We know that this does not work well—at least, not if you want true commitment from the members of your team, the kind where they really, genuinely care about the results. And why is commitment to results so vitally important? Because with employee commitment comes shared ownership of the solution.

Without shared ownership of a solution, then it's just *your* solution, and if it doesn't work, then *your* solution did not work. With employee commitment and caring about results, the employees are encouraged to take the extra step.

After all, that's what owners do.

So to get commitment, leaders need to stop talking at some point during the 20 minutes of coaching and get employees involved—meaning that *they* talk and *you* listen! Are you actually ready for that? Can you be a big enough leader to put aside what you know about the solution and provide ways for your employee(s) to discover it for themselves? This can be challenging, I know, especially when the solution is right there on the tip of your tongue.

Pull energy can help.

Pull energy will open up the conversation and create a free exchange of ideas and understanding—a two-way conversation. You are not just talking at them, giving them orders and reasons—no one will enjoy that. And what's more, that isn't the best utilization of your resources.

You have an employee here, at your disposal, completely ready to absorb or enlighten, for 20 uninterrupted minutes. Who is to say what this employee might add to the conversation? Who is to say what solution might come as a result of this employee's understanding of the problem?

The 20-Minute Leader knows that his or her solution is only one part of the equation; opening up the floor, one employee at a time, is a critically effective means of canvassing the team for unique, effective solutions.

So you are smart, you have a lot to say, you've been around the block, and wisdom and experience are indeed priceless, but now you need to stop, ask questions, and listen. This is you learning, adapting, and growing; this is you being not just the best leader for the job, but also the leader who listens for other ways to get the job done. You must demonstrate that you can do this in real time, and sometimes it will take real discipline and, of course, patience.

The 20-Minute Coaching Conversation goes against everything we've been taught in business school: take over, lead, distribute, challenge, persuade, tell, control, disseminate, instruct, and so on. Instead, you receive, listen, discuss, emphasize, learn, and value; it's beneficial, but it's far from natural—at least, at first.

With Pull behavior, you actively engage the employee, and together you create solutions. The Pull behaviors you may use during your 20-Minute Coaching Conversation are:

1. *Asking open-ended questions.* Don't fudge this golden opportunity by hedging your bets or asking multiple-choice questions designed merely to bring the employee to your point of view. Instead, ask truly open-ended questions like, "What are *your* thoughts?" or "What would *you* do to solve this?" This forces you to sit back and listen even as it forces the employee to think for him- or herself.

2. *Active listening.* Just as you are not used to listening, your employees most likely will find it a challenge to speak openly. They are looking to you for clues and guidance, and if you are sitting there with a blank expression and letting them talk for 20 minutes un-interrupted, you are merely inviting them to babble. Instead, guide the discussion through active listening. Say things like, "So what you're saying is . . ." or "Here is what I am understanding about your idea." This gently prods the employee to keep going without either shutting him or her down or not providing any guidance at all.

3. *Drill-down questions.* A third type of Pull behavior is re-ferred to as drilling down; this means that you guide a little more selectively by getting to the heart of the matter through a series of leading questions that keep the conversation on track while still eliciting specific employee responses. So you might say something like, "If we need this by next Monday, how would you approach it?" or "What is it about Section Two that worries you?" This way, you are still in a leadership position, and the

employee is still offering his or her solid, unique, and personal perspective.

These are behaviors that build relationships and understanding, but they must be done in a purposeful and sincere way if they are to be effective. It is through these Pull behaviors that leaders demonstrate that they have a real interest in the problems that the employees are facing, that they really understand and care about resolving these issues together.

No doubt you will feel the familiar tug of old ideas nagging at you during your first few 20-Minute Coaching Conversations; that is to be expected. However, you must resist the temptation of old habits and have the discipline to make a change if you are truly going to be a 20-Minute Leader.

Merely talking for 20 minutes and asking for input during the last 60 seconds won't cut it; that is merely paying lip service to the idea that you can effectively lead through conversation. In fact, that's not a conversation at all. (See the discussion of disruptive conversations in the Introduction.)

It's not a conversation if only one person is talking.

—Charles Schwab

Fearing the Pull

Kathleen initially resisted the idea of using these Pull behaviors, and with good reason. After all, during her 15-year career at a large semiconductor company, she had fought hard to establish herself as a tough manager—at least as tough as her mostly male colleagues. At team meetings, her reputation reinforced her drive to succeed in a no-nonsense, take-no-prisoners style. But recently, her rigid communication style had been failing her in an unexpected way.

The team's performance had been steadily falling off, and the new ideas that had always seemed to be part of her team meetings were suddenly nonexistent. One of Kathleen's most trusted allies, a 30-year veteran who was about to retire, gave Kathleen a bit of advice at his retirement luncheon.

"You don't really invite people to contribute," he said in confidence. "I think your team is feeling like they are just there to follow your orders. If people don't feel like they are part of something, then they have no skin in the game. And everyone needs to feel like they have a contribution to make. That's what kept me going all these years; anytime I stopped believing that, I just got myself on another team—fast."

Kathleen pondered the words for days after her colleague retired. "But won't using more listening and questioning send the wrong signal to my team?" Kathleen wondered one sleepless night. "Won't that convey the message that I'm unsure and looking for help?"

When I spoke with Kathleen over a coffee about her feelings on using more Pull behaviors in her meetings and with her coaching, she admitted that she had consciously hidden this part of herself at work. Early on, Kathleen had believed that in order to be respected, she needed to always appear as a tough manager to her counterparts and teams; she needed to be always smart and always in the know. That tough, no-nonsense, almost combative style became her own personal brand.

I understood her motivations, but I pointed out that this style was no longer getting results and suggested that a new brand was needed. Trying Pull behaviors, I pointed out, could work more effectively than what she'd been doing. Despite her reservations, Kathleen decided to give it a try. She soon found that these Pull behaviors created an openness to her meetings, and that people were beginning to speak with more candor. And she felt a sense of relief when new ideas began to flow again and coaching actually became easier. Suddenly, everyone had a stake in the results. As her colleague had suggested, they now had skin in the game.

Yes, Kathleen still fell back into her old habits once in a while, but now she knew the difference between *dictating answers* and *inviting participation. And* she was making more and more choices for flexibility between her Push and Pull behavior use.

It was important for Kathleen to have choices; she now knew that both Push and Pull behaviors were effective under specific circumstances. Rather than being a one-trick pony as a dictator, she now knew that she could take one hat off when it wasn't working and use the other to be more effective as the proper conditions arose.

While some leaders resist the Push energy as being too confrontational, other leaders (like Kathleen) look at the Pull behaviors as being too soft! And as a leader, you must understand that listening and questioning don't get you anywhere directly—they are indirect and will take some patience on the leader's part.

So some leaders fear the Push; others fear the Pull. To me, that's fine; fear is a sign of change, and in this case the change is for the better. Both Push and Pull behaviors help the leader and the employee actively engage with each other. The key is to be prepared to both Push and Pull appropriately in your 20-Minute Meeting.

Like Kathleen, you now have choices, and, like Kathleen and so many other effective 20-Minute Leaders, you must learn to get a feel for which behaviors to use—and when. That is why the 20-Minute Coaching Conversation is structured to provide for an initial assessment period during which you can take your time, regroup, reassess, and respond appropriately.

Just as some employees respond better to a firmer, more decisive leader, others flourish when they are given latitude for autonomy and participation. Which is which? This is up to you to decide, of course, and there's no better way than by mapping out a refreshing and effective 20-Minute Coaching Conversation.

How? Where should you spend the most time, in what way, and for how long? Don't worry; you too can use these 20 minutes for maximum effect when you simply divvy up the time in the way that leads to the best results. For example, in the 20-Minute Leader time frame, you would plan the time something like this:

- *Expectations and importance.* Give yourself 1 to 3 minutes to state your expectations and why they are important (using Push behaviors as your guide).
- *Questioning and listening.* Next, take 4 to 10 minutes to do your questioning and listening (using Pull behaviors as your guide).
- *Solution and agreement.* Finally, schedule the last 5 to 7 minutes to select a solution and get agreement (using both energies).

How might this scenario look in real life? Let's go back to Jim and Sharon and see how their conversation might look if the Pull energy we just discovered were included. Let's assume that Sharon (you remember Sharon from our discussion of Push behavior) finally got her expectations on the table about needing Jim's report by Tuesday no later than 3 p.m.

"Well, that's going to be pretty tough," Jim insists when Sharon finally asserts with him.

Sharon now decides to ask an open-ended question to elicit more information from Jim. "What will make that tough for you?"

Jim reminds Sharon, "I'm short-handed; one analyst is on vacation."

Sharon listens actively and responds, "So you're saying that the main problem is that one of your folks is out? And that's going to slow things down?"

Jim responds, "Yes, but it's not just that. Sometimes we don't get all the data we need from Ben's group, and we need to go back and get more and clarify with Ben what we are missing. It takes three or four days to get it complete enough to work with."

Sharon drills down a little by asking, "How might you speed that up?"

Jim admits, "I'm not sure."

Sharon drills down just a little farther by asking, "What might we try if we need to get it by this Tuesday?"

Jim answers, "Well, we could just give you the raw data without checking for completed data from Ben's group."

Sharon encourages while still continuing to Pull. "Okay, that's one idea," she compliments. "What else?"

Jim thinks for a second before replying, "Well, I guess I could spend more time Friday afternoon and ask my remaining analyst to stay an hour later to work with me."

Sharon moves to wrap up her conversation through solution and agreement. "Jim, I think we have a couple of ideas, at least, for solving this for this week. How can I help you?"

Ideally, Jim would offer some concrete solutions to which Sharon could respond. Of course, not *every* conversation will go this smoothly, regardless of whether you use Push or Pull behaviors. However, the Pull behaviors give the leader the best opportunity to invite the employee into the process. In so doing, the leader provides real ownership for the employee.

We also find that once the leader states his or her expectations (Push), the employee will need to Push back. It's very natural for people to feel the need to push back on expectations—and tell you why your expectation is a problem or why your reasons may not make sense to them. As Jim pushes back to Sharon, "I'm short-handed; one analyst is on vacation."

Expect your employees to push back!

Invite them to push back!

Then solve the issues together!

Employees really get something from good, tight coaching in this critical time frame:

1. *Immediate* clarity on what you want when you let them know that they are missing the target (or how to take performance to a higher level)
2. *Immediate* understanding that you're having this conversation because you want them to be successful
3. An *immediate* invitation by you for the employees to participate in solving the issue (or how to take their performance to the next level)
4. An *immediate* agreement on the next steps: who, what, where, when, and how this will be followed up
5. An *immediate* sense of relief on the part of both parties that they are on the same page or at least open to a two-way conversation
6. *Immediate* confidence that the leader knows what success looks like and understands what the employees are up against when trying to make changes in performance

When Push Meets Pull—and Vice Versa: Two Heads Are Better than One

The behaviors that we find most effective in the 20-Minute Coaching Conversation are a combination of Push and Pull energies: knowing when to demand and expect and knowing when to question, poke, and prod work best when they are used together at various appropriate times. However, within those two arenas, there are seven conversational qualities that will be most important for the leader:

Push

1. *Asserting* what you think and what you want
2. *Suggesting*—putting ideas and recommendations on the table for discussion
3. *Consequences*—letting the employee know what is at stake with change or lack of change
4. *Providing reasons*—stating why this issue is important and why are we talking about it

Pull

5. *Asking open-ended questions*—inviting the other into the conversation
6. *Focused questions*—drilling down to get more specific information
7. *Listening*—checking understanding and building mutual respect

You can clearly see how suggesting, consequences, and providing reasons fit well beneath the larger heading of Push behaviors, while focused questions and listening enhance the idea of Pull behaviors. But how will you know when to use Push or Pull—or both? Careful planning is the key. To prepare for your coaching meeting, we recommend the Five-Minute Planning Worksheet:

The Five-Minute "Positive Preparation" Worksheet

To best identify which behavior(s) will be the most effective, you need to take five minutes to clear your head of all the things that have been going on during the day and focus on the 20-Minute Conversation with your employee. I call this Five-Minute Positive Preparation, and, although it's short, it's absolutely vital to pulling off an effective 20-Minute Coaching Conversation.

Remember, the best part about these conversations will happen spontaneously when an employee "gets it" and lets loose with a new idea, a solution, or just a simple piece of information; but these aren't mere improvisations.

Regardless of whether you use Push or Pull behaviors and the variety of tactics that go with each (discussed earlier), you are in control of the conversation, and, as we all know, careful control takes careful planning. Knowing what questions to ask and when gives you that control—and five minutes of careful planning is well worth the initial investment for the many returns to follow.

When managers take the time to prepare—just five minutes—the message they are sending is that *this conversation matters*. What you are saying to the employee is, "I have thought about you and what you need in order to be more successful." This is encouragement, direction, and focus in 15 words or less.

Your Five-Minute Positive Preparation will be to use a simple three-step model:

1. *Identify.*
2. *Involve.*
3. *Initiate.*

Get to know these three steps because they will be vital in every conversation you have from now on. In fact, *every* 20-Minute Leadership Conversation that we will explore in this book will revolve around these three steps. What does each entail? Let's consider them individually and find out:

1. *Identify.* Why are we having this conversation? For coaching, we want to identify the issues and barriers to the desired performance or improved performance.
2. *Involve.* How can we seek improvement and solutions together?
3. *Initiate.* What are the action steps to take next? What is our agreement to change?

The process will look like this:

- *Step 1: Identify.* Make a clear statement of the issue.
  — *Assert:* "I want to talk about Friday's deadlines. . . ."
  — *Provide reasons:* "The two reasons why I need you to meet this deadline are . . ."
  — *Consequences:* "I want you to know the downside impact of not meeting the deadline. . . ."

- *Step 2: Involve.* Gather information, concerns, and the point of view of the employee
  — *Ask open-ended questions:* "What do you think about this?" or "What is getting in the way?"
  — *Summarize:* Listen, then restate what you have understood your employee to be saying. "What I have understood about your situation is . . ." or, "So you're saying that . . ."
  — *Ask focused questions:* "Would you tell me more about . . . ?" or, "How exactly does the process work?" or, "What are your ideas to improve this?"
- *Step 3: Initiate.* Agree on a new course of action.
  — *Suggest:* "Here is an idea . . ." or, "Let's take your idea and add this to it . . ."
  — *Assert:* "This is what I would like to try" or, "I would like you to agree to this first."
  — *Suggest:* "Let's meet again next week to follow up."

Once leaders have used this three-step model several times, planning for a 20-Minute Coaching Conversation becomes very easy. In fact, following up with our workshop participants has shown us that three months after learning this three-step model, 68 percent are still using it effectively. They report that in many cases they have even improved on the 20-minute time frame, getting these coaching conversations done in less time—15 minutes in some cases. Taking 5 minutes to prepare really pays off in more effective and efficient conversations and outcomes.

Good communication is not magic, it's mechanics, it only seems like magic after you've done it a hundred times.

—Ron Sacchi

It's What You Say That Counts

As one executive informed me, "People don't hear what we think they hear—they have all sorts of ways of interpreting what we think is our clear communication. Have you ever had a roommate?" he asked me.

"Of course," I responded.

"Well," he continued, "how many different ways are there to define 'clean'? If you have four people sharing a house, like my son in college does right now, there are four different meanings for the word *clean*!!"

There really is a miscommunication going on here, and bridging that communication gap is actually one of the most important aspects of coaching. In fact, many employees believe that they are doing what their bosses want, only to be surprised when they get feedback that they have missed the mark.

So, if miscommunication is the *biggest* complaint employees have about their leaders, what's the second? Feedback. That's right; feedback is the second-biggest complaint that employees have about their so-called leaders. The complaint is either that they just don't get feedback, period, or that they don't get enough or in a positive and constructive way.

Okay, this isn't rocket science; it's harder then rocket science!

A study at Michigan State University School of Business asserts that the absence of good, constructive feedback prompts a demand for more pay and benefits. Why? Because pay and benefits becomes the prime measuring stick for success in the job.

So it is important for both parties to master what I call the feedback vacuum. What's missing is realistic conversations about how employees are doing in relationship to the goals to be achieved. What happens in this "feedback vacuum" is that employees think everything is okay, and say to themselves, "If I get a raise, that will give me the feedback that everything is all right with my work."

What's the solution? One thing: courage.

Courage on the part of the leaders is also missing, the courage and know-how that give the leader the ability to tell the truth in a way that helps others succeed. And this is a two-way street. Employees aren't getting feedback about their performance, but neither are leaders getting the feedback that they need.

The solution is effective coaching.

How True Leaders Coach Effectively

One of my best aerospace clients asked me to speak with Beth, a talented young leader who had just taken on a new product team. Beth wanted more commitment from several members of her group, especially Jon, a Gen-Xer just out of graduate school who had a lot of potential, but did not seem to "get it."

"How do I get that real commitment?" she asked during our initial meeting. "You know, the kind where people take the extra step."

"You can't get commitment," I informed her, "because you have not defined what it is. What does *commitment* mean to you?" I asked her.

"Well," she explained, "someone who is involved, someone who does what is necessary."

"Is that what you told Jon?" I asked. "If so, then he is probably very confused."

Beth needed to define the word *commitment* in precise behavioral terms that left nothing to the imagination. Before asking it of others, she first had to define it for herself: what does it look like, and how will you see it and measure it?

"Okay," she responded when I put these questions to her, "for one thing, he would show up at team meetings on time."

This was a great start. "Okay," I suggested. "Why don't you start with that expectation at your next coaching meeting?"

A week went by, and Beth and I spoke again. "So," I asked, "what happened with Jon? Success?"

"Almost," she said. "Jon did show up on time for this week's team meeting, but he sat way in the back of the room, opened up his laptop, and did e-mails for the entire meeting. At least, I think it was e-mails; he could have been updating his Facebook page!!"

My diagnosis was easier this time; clearly, Beth had given Jon only *part* of the expectation involving the commitment she needed.

"Beth, what exactly do you want Jon to do that is specific, behavioral, and measurable?" I asked.

Beth thought for a moment and then replied, "I want Jon to come to the meeting on time, sit near the front, not open his laptop, ask at least three questions about what others are reporting on, and be prepared to give the other members of the team a three-minute status report on his project and let the others know at least one thing he needs help on now!"

I smiled and said, "If that's what commitment looks like to you, Beth, and you communicate it like that to Jon, I bet you're going to get it." No doubt, she did!

Remember that clarity is key in making these brief but effective conversations stand out. The idea is not to make meetings shorter in order to get them over with, but to use each of your 20 minutes that much more effectively. That is why the process is carefully mapped out for you; to wit, each 20-Minute Conversation is built around a three-step process—*identify*, *involve*, and *initiate*—with each step addressing specific performance questions. So here again is my simple three-step formula for the 20-Minute Coaching Conversation:

1. *Identify:* What exactly do you need, and what exactly have you been getting?
2. *Involve:* What does that employee think, and what ideas does he have?
3. *Initiate:* What do we agree to do, and when will we follow up?

How important is feedback? A great deal of research has been done regarding feedback processes (or the lack of them, even with managers who have been at it for 20 years or more). The Center for Creative Leadership believes that the absence of clear, straightforward feedback helps many managers fail at all levels of the process, from managing their own careers to helping their direct reports succeed.

Formal feedback and coaching need to take place at the appropriate time of the year (or several times throughout), but it's really the informal day-to-day and week-to-week quick, corrective conversations that keep employees from wasting valuable time chasing unproductive activity, leading to frustration on the part of both parties and ultimately disappointment in the long run.

It's not enough to be busy. The question is: What are you busy about?

—Henry David Thoreau

You Don't Know Jack (but I Do!)

If the previous scenario sounds familiar, then you're going to love Jack. Jack is not a real person, but the situations he encounters—and how they are often handled—will seem very real to you. That's because Jack is a combination of nearly every new leader I've ever encountered, so I'm using him as a shining example of how *not* to lead.

But don't worry; there's hope for Jack, because as he learns how to coach, motivate, and mentor, he will discover the absolute joy of leading effectively. My hope is that, along the way, so will you:

Jack opened the door to his new office. It even smelled new. Everything was clean and fresh, just the way Jack was feeling about his new role as manager of the new product development team. The team consisted of ten highly motivated, highly educated, highly recruited, and highly paid professionals—and did I say highly independent minded too? They all reported to Jack, a successful project manager who had built a great reputation as a can-do project leader.

Yes, indeed, this was his chance to show what he could do leading an ongoing, high-powered team. Finally, he had been awarded the promotion that had been promised to him for the past 18 months, one that would be a great step on his path to a directorship. Little did he know that his challenge of managing this type of team had just begun.

First off, Ben, the best engineer on the team, announced in their one-on-one meeting later that week that he would be leaving the team! This was the most creative and innovation-minded employee that Jack had. What's more, Jack had been counting on Ben to be a team leader, someone that other members of the team would look up to and admire.

"But why?" Jack asked Ben, hoping that it wouldn't sound as if he was begging the man to stay! "I just took over the leadership here, and I'm planning on lots of

challenging work and a leadership position for you in the near future."

The departing engineer shrugged and confessed, "I really can't wait around for that anymore; it seems like I've always been waiting forever. And I really need some clean wins. Nothing on this team ever seems to go from A to Z; we never have a successful launch of a new product.

"Okay, I don't mean ever, but it seems like we are always surprised by something that we did not know. No one, from the manager on up, ever gives us ongoing feedback on how we are doing, so we guess—and guessing is just not good enough for me anymore, so I've got a position on a new team."

While he thanked the man for his candid admission, Jack had a bad feeling about this.

What had he walked into?

Planning is as normal to the process of success as its absence is to the process of failure.

—Robin Sieger

Now Try This . . .

Can you feel Jack's pain? I certainly can. But the first rule of leadership is to read between the lines, and if Jack had listened closely to Ben, his departing engineer, rather than cursing his own fate, he would have discovered a gold mine of helpful information. Why, Ben was basically telling him how to solve the problem: give feedback! Go along a straight line, from A to Z. Publish expectations; let us know what is required. Give us deadlines and input and . . . feedback!

But Jack *didn't* listen. And Jack's not alone; few leaders listen effectively. That is why it is important for you as a leader to understand that you need coaching conversations. Why coaching conversations? Why not? Seriously, coaching conversations have a lot to offer. Here are just some of the rewards you get when you use coaching conversations effectively:

1. More challenging goals and projects
2. Encouragement to set high standards and foster an attitude of being the best
3. Help in identifying problem issues and new creative options
4. More direct feedback and ideas on how to succeed
5. More sharing of expertise and experience in order to perform current tasks better

When should you use coaching conversations? Here is a quick primer.

Use Coaching If . . .

-   You want to encourage individual task completion and goal achievement.

- You want to enhance performance through feedback on what's working and what's not working as well.
- An individual's job performance consistently lags for a period of time.
- An individual needs a quick course correction to keep her job performance on track.
- It's time to create annual development goals as part of performance management (for the team and for individuals).

WORKSHEET I

COACHING

The three parts of the 20-Minute Coaching Conversation are:

1. *Identify issues.* Successful coaches use specific language and behaviors to address feedback and important issues; they state expectations clearly. *Assert* with statements like, "What I need from you is . . . " or, "What I think of your performance is . . ." Don't beat around the bush. If you're uncomfortable being this direct, plan it out ahead of time or practice first; above all, be prepared.

2. *Involve the other.* Get the employee involved in the conversation. Ask open-ended questions—in other words, questions that do not have a yes or no answer. "What is getting in the way of completing the report?" Listen deeply for the answer, then check for understanding by summarizing *exactly* what you think the employee is saying. Why? Simple: this gives evidence not only of hear-

ing the employee's concerns but also of understanding those concerns. For example: "So, you're saying that you are not getting the data on time." Involvement will help you get a commitment to resolving the issues and moving forward to a new course of action, and you will probably learn something about the situation that will need to be addressed in the next step. "What do you think your options are at this point?" "What else might be possible?" Open-ended questions like these are valuable because it's important to get the employee's ideas on how to move forward. By the way, have your ideas ready too, so that together you are helping to solve the issues.

3. *Initiate action.* Make suggestions based on your ideas and the employee's that have been generated together. What is the appropriate action or steps to be taken? What will you do—and what will the employee do—*first* to correct the issue discussed? To find out, have an informal contract with the employee to discuss when, where, and how. Then ask yourself, "When will I follow up? What are the next steps?" Finally, offer solutions to initiate action: "Here are my suggestions for next steps" or "Let's try this for our first step in correcting this issue." Both parties need to be absolutely clear on what will happen next.

Nothing astonishes men so much as common sense and plain dealing.

—Ralph Waldo Emerson

WORKSHEET 2

THE PROCESS

Here is a template for your first 20-Minute Coaching Conversation.

Step 1: Identify—Clear Statement of Issue

- *Assert.* "I want to talk about Friday's deadlines."
- *Provide rationale.* "The two reasons for this are . . ."
- *Identify consequences.* "I want you to know that the downside impact is . . ."

Step 2: Involve—Gather Information and Concerns

- *Ask open-ended questions.* "What do you think about this?"
- *Summarize.* "What I understand you're saying is . . ."
- *Ask focused questions.* "Can you tell me more about . . . ?"
- *Suggest.* "One idea is to do it like this . . ."

Step 3: Initiate—Agree on New Course of Action

- *Assert.* "I would like to try this . . ."
- *Suggest.* "I suggest we talk again on . . ."

WORKSHEET 3

YOUR FIVE-MINUTE PLANNING TO-DO LIST

Before you meet with your employee, it is important that you spend five minutes preparing. Use this worksheet as a guide to make this planning time even more effective:

1. *Identify:* What is the main issue to be discussed?

    _____

    • What do you need from the employee?

    • Why is it important?

    _____

    • What are the consequences if it is not done?

2. *Involve:* Questions to ask; get ideas together:

    _____

    • Listening responses?

    _____

3. *Initiate:* What do you think the next steps will be?

    _____

    • Agreements, when and how to follow up?

    _____

CHAPTER 2

HOW TO USE FEEDBACK FOR REAL SUCCESS

Janice, one of my favorite tennis partners, has a wicked backhand, but (forgive me, Janice) an even greater sense of humor. Just the other day she offered the following suggestion: "Why don't we try and play without the tennis net today? I mean, it only gets in the way. And while we're at it, let's ignore the lines on the court; they only give us bad news. We could have a much more enjoyable game if we just took out these distractions. No net, no lines; now, *that's* positive tennis."

And, of course, this would be totally meaningless tennis!

While it occasionally gets in the way of what would otherwise surely be another ace serve, the net provides us with immediate feedback: if the ball does not go over the net but goes into the net, we know that we must adjust our shot. In this case, we need to hit the ball higher. So, not having a net might be fun for a minute, but it will make the game pointless.

And, of course, the court lines tell us whether a ball is in or out. There is no equivocating with such instantaneous feedback; the ball simply either lands inside the lines to warrant another return or lands decidedly out of the court. Without such lines, most tennis games would dissolve into endless shouting matches over "it was in," "no, it was out," and no one would ever score a single point.

So consider the netless, line-free tennis match: no one will be awarded points, there are no winners and no losers—the game would soon become boring and, what's worse, pointless. Serious tennis enthusiasts are out there to play, to get exercise, and to get the satisfaction of a game well played. Winning or losing may not be the ultimate goal, but who doesn't walk off the court with a spring in their step after winning a round? Who doesn't vow to do just a little better, work just a little harder next time, after they lose?

Without the feedback needed to know good shots from bad, in from out, we will never feel a sense of accomplishment and will simply be operating in the dark. It really won't matter how we hit the ball—there will be no measurement of in or out, good or bad, win or loss. As a result, no one will really care all that much about where the ball lands.

I know this isn't a sports book, but, sadly, lots of good people in our organizations today are playing tennis with no net and no lines. We don't let them know how to win, so they simply show up to work and bat the ball back and forth all day, with no real passion, purpose, or payoff.

We simply can't breed top performers with low (or no) expectations. Most people feel—and few would be wrong—that they are not getting paid for hitting good shots or getting good results. What *are* they getting paid for? Basically, they are getting paid for simply hitting balls. It doesn't really matter where the balls land because we don't have clear lines on the court, so as a result the people don't really know when a ball is in and when it is out. We need feedback to make work meaningful, to feel accomplishment when we hit our own goals.

Finding Success with Feedback

One of my engineering participants at an aerospace company recently shared with me that the word *"feedback"* first came into our everyday language some time in the 1960s. During the first space shot to put a man on the moon, as schoolchildren we had a chance to watch the action unfold on TV.

"Feedback" was the word they used at Cape Kennedy to tell us whether the rocket was on track or off track. It's really an electronics word. And as the rocket was speeding toward the moon, the engineers at Cape Canaveral had to make adjustments. More than 2,000 adjustments had to be made so that the rocket would hit its target successfully, or it would miss its orbit around the moon.

Feedback is used to help people be successful in meeting their goals—and the mindset of the leader must communicate that attitude. People need to believe that the 20-Minute Coaching Conversation is intended to help them be more successful.

Employees need to have a level of trust in the leader—to feel that the leader has their best interests at heart, that the reason for these 20 minutes is to make sure that the employee and ultimately the team have the best chance of success.

Unfortunately, there is a problem with the very word *"feedback."* It has been misused, abused, misunderstood, and overplayed. It has been a "red flag" word for many years now. Employees at every level of the organization have been burned by this word, largely by bosses who don't know how to give it with "good will," empathy, compassion, or, for that matter, an eye for results Many bosses use feedback to simply dump bad news on people—especially employees—without giving any clear action steps to be taken in the future so that the employees have a chance for success.

Just as we need nets and lines to make tennis more competitive and rewarding, those parameters must be reasonable if we are to feel any measure of success. Leaders who give feedback incorrectly, negatively, or even recklessly are guilty of making their nets too high and their lines too close; no one can play their best when they're being hemmed in or squared off.

"It is much more difficult to measure non-performance than performance."

—Harold S. Geneen

"Feedback" by Any Other Name . . .

One of the first things I tell leaders is to drop the word *"feedback"* altogether from the 20-Minute Coaching Conversation. In our research, we have found that *85 percent* of the participants in our workshops have a negative reaction to the word itself.

Someone in their past has used the word to inflict fear and pain—and now the word itself instantly sets off feelings and thoughts that bad news will be communicated, regardless of whether the feedback itself is good or bad.

When asked what other words could be substituted for the word "*feedback*," here is what people came up with:

- "Here are my ideas . . ."
- "These are my thoughts . . ."
- "This is what I have observed . . ."
- "This is my point of view . . ."
- "Here is my input . . ."

If you'll notice, this list contains almost anything *but* "feedback"!

In research on executive traits, University of Chicago professors Steven Kaplan, Mark Klebanov, and Morton Sorenson asked the question, "What are the traits that chief executives of successful companies share?" Their findings point to several traits, including a persistence in purpose, an efficiency in execution, and the ability to communicate high standards.

Whatever we choose to call it, the use of feedback that is clear and efficient, and that is delivered in a consistent and persistent format, is critical to the leader's success. In order for a 20-Minute Coaching Conversation to encompass these leadership traits, the leader must be clear in his or her preparation.

Before giving, or receiving, feedback, it is necessary to answer these questions: "What will the feedback look like and sound like, and what should we expect from each other in the future? What can we do to make these corrective steps happen so that both of us can be more successful?"

Marshall Goldsmith, noted executive coach, talks about his alternative to feedback, which he calls "FeedForward." The idea is not to look back in order to judge past deeds, but instead to focus on the future and on what can be done to correct, encourage, or improve performance in the days, weeks, and months ahead.

While doing away with the term "*feedback*," we must not forget its ultimate purpose: knowledge—knowledge about the employee's performance and your expectations, and wisdom about what is needed to produce results and garner success.

It is very important for an employee to feel that there is a new step or a next step that gets him closer to the goal or desired performance; that is the driving principle of feedback. After all, what are we trying to do here if not get better results that will serve everybody? Forget about looking back at the past to place blame or find fault. Instead, focus on the future and what will be done to move forward.

Real Workplace Stories of Ineffective Feedback and the Damage It Can Do

Clearly it is important to give feedback—the more the better. More than 40 percent of people don't feel that they get any feedback, according to Matthew Kelly, using research done by Chicago-based Floyd Consulting. More than 70 percent say that they don't get enough feedback to be successful at their jobs.

This is critical information; these are red flags to be observed—and avoided—in every organization. Remember, people don't fail because they're not good at their jobs. People fail because *they don't know how to succeed.*

According to one HR manager at an insurance company I recently spoke with, "I watched two new IT engineers slowly lose all motivation, not long after they were hired. They simply got no signal from their manager on what they were doing right, let alone any corrective information on how to improve. They told me that they just came to the conclusion that no one really cared. They figured the company was really just paying for someone to show up to work and meeting goals was 'not that important.' They were [already] looking around for something better."

Think of the lost opportunities for feedback these two employees were experiencing (not to mention the HR manager). All three knew what the problem was, but no one wanted to address it. Or, perhaps, none of them knew *how* to address it. Where was the net for them to hit into, around, or over? Where were the lines to keep them in bounds and let them know when they were "in" or "out"?

More specifically, I wonder what "better" looked like to these employees. I assume that it was probably along the lines of more feedback, more direction, more constructive criticism, and more involvement. The "better" that these employees were looking for would have been right under their noses, if only their leaders could—or would—have provided it.

All things considered, I find this to be a hopeful story. Why? Simple: because all three of the individuals involved were highly intelligent, highly capable people who should have been working effectively. Mixed signals from above and below created a workplace that was not conducive to productivity; work became a tennis match with no nets, no lines, and no buy-in. Why show up at all when everyone is merely going through the motions, with no in or out, win or loss? Priorities merely needed to be communicated to all parties; that was the "better" these employees were looking for—and could easily have gotten with just a few 20-Minute Coaching Conversations.

A junior engineer at a high-tech company recently told me, "My boss travels a lot, and when he is in town, he mostly catches up with meetings with upper management, then it's off to Asia again. If I can get him for a quick meeting just to check on the status of things, I'm lucky.

"Then I found out that priorities had changed and I had been spending way too much time on a project that will be dropped soon. I felt like I had wasted my time, and I was disappointed in my boss for not keeping me up to date and in the loop. Then he rated me lower on my appraisal last month; that's just not fair."

This is a common scenario of leaders feeling frustrated because they are not given the tools needed to lead. If this leader is confused and bemused by his boss, what do you think his employees feel on a daily basis? What kind of messages are they getting?

Four Best Ways to Prepare for Your Feedback

To have a quick 20-Minute Coaching Conversation, the leader must be able and willing to get the message out there quickly, and to have the courage to be this direct. Much of coaching is going to require clear, clean feedback, and *feedback* is one of those words that sends chills down the back of most leaders— and most employees as well.

People generally don't know how to deliver feedback well— or, for that matter, how to take it well. Feedback typically creates stress for the leader who is not comfortable with giving it and fear in the employee who doesn't handle feedback well. (Consider those 85 percent of workshop participants who vehemently opposed the idea of feedback!) So it takes preparation and courage to do both, particularly in a 20-Minute Coaching Conversation.

To master the art of giving and receiving feedback, let's first examine a quick formula for feedback preparation. Leaders can follow these four steps to get clear on what it is they need to do, thereby creating an actionable and repeatable template for future 20-Minute Coaching Conversations:

- *Step 1: Identify the problem.* Objectively state what you are seeing or hearing. For instance, say something nonpersonal like, "Your reports are coming in later and later. Case in point: the Monday morning report came in late Tuesday afternoon." This part of the conversation is neither a personal condemnation nor a judgment call—merely a fact that the employee can't dispute. The objective statement is clear: your reports aren't being turned in on time. Steps 2 through 4 work to resolve this statement.

- *Step 2: State the repercussions.* Explain the problem by giving the reasons why this performance is not working for you and what opportunities are being missed (or what problems are occurring) because of this behavior. "Because of the tardiness of your reports, I'm missing the data for my Monday afternoon one-on-one with my boss. And I'm feeling anxious and embarrassed that I don't have it ready on time." Now the employee knows why you are having this discussion and how it is affecting you both. This visualization—you going into your boss hat in hand because of the employee's tardiness—represents a clear consequence of his or her behavior.

- *Step 3: Define your deliverables.* Expectations for what changes are desired need to be stated clearly and specifically: "What I need is to have your report no later than noon on Mondays." This is a clear, concise deliverable that the employee should have no problem either understanding or delivering. Often employees devolve rather than evolve; they gradually slip into a way of doing things more slowly or less effectively because they are allowed to by (you guessed it) lack of specific feedback. Now the employee has no excuse; the deliverable is clear, specific, and expected.

- *Step 4: Name the consequences of this behavior.* State clearly that there is a consequence for the behavior that is creating this conversation. What will happen as a result of your not getting your expectations met? What payoffs or penalties will there be for the person or the team for accepting or rejecting your expectations for change? You don't need to threaten the person; however, he does need a clear idea of the downside of not changing his performance. For instance, "I would like to move you on to some new learning opportunities; however, I'm hesitant because I'm not getting what I need now." Now the team member has a choice: step up and receive the desired benefits, or ignore them and suffer the consequences through missed opportunities and potential.

Consider this feedback exercise good practice in preparing for the 20-Minute Coaching Conversation. The four steps just discussed are really to allow you, the leader, to get your mindset clear concerning exactly what you need, what you think, and the language that you need in order to deliver the message best before you actually deliver it.

It's not a script, per se, because every conversation is different; every conversation should be different. Consider it more of a template, a rhythm that every instance of feedback should follow: *identify, state, define,* and *name.* When you follow this pattern consistently and effectively, feedback will become less of a red flag and more of an opportunity for you and your team to excel together.

Now Try This

One of the biggest challenges of giving feedback, particularly if you're not used to it, is being specific. This worksheet will help you think about whom you owe feedback to and help you plan for this 20-Minute Coaching Conversation.

1. Here is what I have seen or heard:

    On the following blank line, state something specific that you have seen or heard that requires feedback, such as reports coming in later and later or work not being done on time.

    _____

2. What are the repercussions of this behavior?

    Now write down a possible repercussion of this behavior *for the company or the department*, such as lost momentum on a project or having to work over the weekend.

    _____

3. Define what you really want.

    On the line below, list specifically what you really want to accomplish as a result of this feedback, e.g., the reports coming in on time or performance improving.

    _____

4. What are the consequences if the behavior stays the same?

    Finally, list a possible consequence of this behavior *for the individual*, such as having to complete his or her reports early from now on and/or to have them approved by a certain date and time.

Characteristics of Great Coaches

- They are focused on performance success.
- They reward success.
- They reward failing less.
- They gain commitment and compliance.
- They know the skills and talents.
- They make feedback constructive.

Tips for the Coaching Conversation

- Stay focused on performance issues.
- Stay future-oriented as much as possible.
- Stay on measurable, observable actions and tasks.
- Stay away from attitudes, personalities, and anything that is not performance-related.
- Stay with "do more" and "do less" as descriptions of behavior.

Coaching Conversation Dos and Don'ts

Dos

- Listen for goals and skills.
- Be specific about future goals.

- Give meaningful feedback.
- Be clear about expectations.
- Ask permission to give advice.

Don'ts

- Assume that people know when they have done well.
- Assume that you know people's skills just from observing them.
- Hoard recognition.
- Wait to give feedback.
- Just say, "Good job" instead of being specific.

Coaching Is Guaranteed to Fail If You

- Do not establish clear performance standards.
- Do not give constructive and on-time feedback on performance.
- Do not express sincere appreciation to individuals for their contribution.

It is very important for employees to feel that there is a new step or a next step that gets them closer to the goal or the desired performance; that is the driving principle of feedback. After all, what are we trying to do here if not get better results that will serve everybody? Forget about looking back to the past to place blame or find fault. Instead, focus on the future and what will be done to move forward.

CHAPTER 3

FOUR BEHAVIORS THAT MAKE COACHING EASY

This past Thanksgiving, I attended a wonderful dinner with family and friends in the spirit of the holiday season. It just so happened that there were two children present at this festive gathering. After dinner, while the rest of us overstuffed adults chose to sit and surreptitiously loosen our belts, the two kids decided to play a game for dessert—one that many of us played in our childhood.

Thomas, a boy of eight, was supposed to hide a piece of delicious after-dinner candy. Jason, nine years old, stood with his eyes closed while Thomas found a difficult place to hide the sweet treat. It was your average game of hide-and-seek, only with one neat twist: neither child could eat the candy until Jason found it.

Now it was time for Jason to begin his hunt, and Thomas would give him clues by saying "Cold," "Warm," "Hot," or some variation thereof. "Warmer" meant that Jason was getting closer. "Hot" meant that Jason was very close to the candy.

As the game progressed, the consultant in me noticed that the feedback Jason was getting was *regular*, *accurate*, and *detailed*. Even when he was going in the wrong direction, he knew it instantly. When Jason took a first step in the wrong direction, Thomas would shout, "Cold!"

And if Jason turned wrong yet again, Thomas would say, "Colder!"

As Jason got closer, Thomas would say, "Warm." The look on Jason's face was pure excitement as Thomas shouted, "Warmer, warmer!" Jason was encouraged—and when "Hot" was shouted, Jason was intense in his search for the candy.

They were working together, and ultimately they succeeded because of one thing: *regular*, *accurate*, and *detailed* feedback:

- The feedback was *regular* because it came in flurries every time Jason made a move. The only way Thomas could get results was to provide the feedback regularly. As he did so, Jason went (for the most part) wherever Thomas directed him to go.
- The feedback was *accurate* in that Thomas never led Jason in the wrong direction. For instance, he never said, "Warm" when Jason was going in the opposite direction or "Cold" when Jason was right on top of the candy.
- Such *detailed* feedback as "Warm," "Warmer," and "Hot" helped Jason know whether he was going in the right direction and, if so, how close he was to reaching his goal.

If Thomas had used only such generalized feedback as "Hot" and "Cold," Jason might never have been able to zero in on the ultimate goal; detailed feedback like "Warmer" and "Colder" let Jason find success through degrees of gray rather than only black and white.

Throughout their game, Jason and Thomas were totally dependent on each other for success. They were both responsible for finding the candy; one's success was the other's success. The feedback and encouragement were constant, each step was important, and success was a mutual agreement.

What can leaders learn from this game? Not that each tiny step must be evaluated with constant shouting from the corner office to the cubicle and back again, but that we are in this together, that your success is my success, and that feedback needs to be even and continuous—specifically, *regular*, *accurate*, and *detailed*.

At each step closer, "Warmer" was a reward—even if the candy was several feet away. Instinctively, to get the joint returns, small successes were recognized and rewarded. People need to feel rewarded for each small step that brings them closer to the goal or performance.

Likewise, an utterance of "Cold" or "Colder" told Jason that he was going in the opposite direction. While at first Jason grew frustrated when he heard that he was heading the wrong way, he soon learned to embrace this negative feedback positively by quickly redirecting his efforts. The more accurately and quickly he responded to "Cold" or "Colder," the less he heard them.

Workers, likewise, are extremely adept at utilizing feedback—any feedback. They learn quickly, and they can respond promptly if the feedback gives them enough information. Often we think we're giving too much or overly detailed feedback when, in actuality, we're saying very little despite spending lots of time, effort, paperwork, e-mails, conference calls, or even words.

Knowing what you want to achieve as an end result is the beginning of giving better feedback. Jason and Thomas were both working toward a shared goal; thus, the feedback could be given quickly and implemented immediately.

> No organization action has more power for motivating employee behavior change than feedback from credible work associates.
>
> —Mark Edwards

Missed Feedback = Missed Opportunities

Feedback is worthwhile, whether it be glowing praise or serious admonitions. The truth is that your people are hungry for any type of feedback, and holding back because you don't want to be the bearer of bad news merely denies them the knowledge they need if they are to perform better and achieve results.

Eric was a VP of finance at a large high-tech company. After a workshop one day, he told me the following story about his lack of ability to spell. In fact, he said, his sixth-grade teacher never rewarded him for failing less.

Every Monday at school, his teacher would hand out 20 spelling words for the class to study for the spelling test the next Friday. But Eric was the kind of student who never really studied, so he would wait until Friday morning, take a quick glance at the list of words for that week, and decide to take his chances on the test. And, of course, he would get the test back on Monday morning with a big "F" on top in red letters. But he said his eye would always go down the page to find about 6 words that he had gotten right.

"Just a good guess," he thought.

Well, every once in a while he would get lucky, and instead of 6 correctly spelled words, he would get 12 words correct. "Outstanding," he thought, "truly amazing." But, of course, there would still be a big red "F" at the top of his test, and there still was not a word from his teacher. Suddenly he was wondering, what if his teacher had recognized his 100 percent improvement (from 6 words correct to 12) and had said to him, "Eric, you have shown a great improvement; you've done a great job. Keep up the good work. I still can't give you a passing grade, *but I know I will be able to soon.*"

With a little encouragement, Eric might have turned out to be a world-class speller!

Reward People for Failing Less

Eric's story points out a key facet of the 20-Minute Coaching Conversation: don't wait for perfection to reward people; *reward people for failing less.* How do people improve? Not with giant leaps or overnight turnarounds, but gradually, one small step at a time.

Great coaches understand that using small goals that move people closer to the ideal performance is the right way to ensure continuing progress. Giving feedback on an ongoing basis, continuing to observe the performance, and helping and encouraging employees to make corrections is key to rewarding people for failing less.

Feedback that is easier to give and easier to hear involves a *four-step* process that creates a solid foundation for *20 Minutes to a Top Performer*:

The Four Steps to Easy Coaching

1. "Do more of this" implies directing a specific action that moves the employee closer to the desired behavior.
2. "Do less of this" is another specific action that calibrates behavior to a more appropriate time frame or frequency.
3. "Keep doing this" contains a compliment that lets an employee know that something is working.
4. "Be prepared to do this" gives people a heads-up about the future and what it will take to provide results.

Whom do you owe some feedback to right now? Do you already have somebody, or even a few somebodies, in mind for a quick 20-Minute Coaching Conversation? Probably you do, and that's because on every team, there are always those employees who do a few things right, but, more often, do lots of little things that need a quick course correction.

Don't wait for an obvious success to give feedback; it can be too long between breakthrough moments or "lucky spelling word choices." Instead, look for opportunities to reward people for failing less; this provides more opportunities for feedback, and the more feedback the employee gets, the less he or she will fail. Everybody wins.

Remember, giving feedback is not about turning a morning person into a night owl or a detail thinker into a visionary thinker. People are who they are; they bring unique skills and valuable, specific talents to the team—that's why you hired them in the first place! Don't try to change anyone's personality—you can't.

What you can do, and what your job is, is to *manage people's behaviors*. This means putting the right people together and letting them work independently, with guidance from you. Feedback is not an opportunity to make captains out of deckhands or activity directors into housekeepers; it's an opportunity for you to steer the ship through the help of these fine, talented people.

Try this simple correction formula to give more feedback more often to those who may not exactly be succeeding, but who could be if you only started rewarding them for failing less. I have found that it is much easier for people to hear this language:

- *Do more of this.* "Kerry, I need you to spend more time training Lin on the new software. Let's ratchet it up to three full hours a week instead of the two you're doing now." This sends two messages: (1) I recognize what you've been doing, and I want you to keep it up, and (2) I need you to do more of it in the near future—specifically, one hour a week more.

- *Do less of this.* "Also, you're coordinating our team meetings with the IT group—a little less time with that. Cut your time back to an hour a week." This statement, likewise, sends two messages: (1) I recognize what you've been doing, and (2) I need you to do less of it in the near future—specifically, one hour a week less.

This language is much easier for people to hear when they are getting feedback, because it means that they are already doing what they should be doing. What you want is for them to do it a little more or a little less. You're not judging their behavior, for once; instead, you're calibrating the behavior. Employees can immediately respond to this both emotionally ("She noticed!") and behaviorally, by doing what you've requested.

"Aren't We Doing Anything Right?!?"

Helen was a regional manager of a fast-food chain restaurant. She had 26 units in her area and 26 managers or direct reports to supervise, visit, and give prompt, professional feedback to; it wasn't always easy.

Helen tried to visit every unit in the region at least once a month. She prided herself on quickly sizing up each unit and what needed to be done. Since she had so many managers and so little time, Helen would walk into the restaurant and immediately see everything that was wrong.

"Let's keep the napkins on this side of the counter," she would tell one store manager.

"This window needs a more thorough cleaning," she might say to another.

Or, "The ketchup pump is dry; let's fill it."

Or even, "Your name tag's on upside down; let's fix that!"

If it's wrong, let's fix it. That was Helen's motto. *And the sooner, the better!* After all, she really didn't have much time, so her feedback needed to be quick and to the point. Then one day, after she had spent 30 minutes with one of her highest-grossing units and best store managers, giving this type of feedback, her manager looked her in the eye and asked, "Aren't we doing *anything* right?"

Helen stopped in her tracks, too stunned for words, and realized that in her zeal to unload everything that needed to be fixed and move on to her next step, she had neglected to say, "Yes, you're doing a lot that is right!"

Imagine if Thomas, one of the children from the opening Thanksgiving hide-and-seek game story, had given Jason *only* negative feedback on his quest for candy: "Cold, cold, colder!" and never any "warm, warmer, hot!" Jason might have found the candy eventually, if he hadn't gotten fed up and quit first!

So we need to add two more parts to the "do more" and "do less" scenario—and those are:

- *Keep doing.* "Your display of this month's specials is perfect! In fact, everyone who comes into the store sees it immediately. Keep doing this. Your sales on this are up 7 percent." This kind of statement lets people know that you know they have been successful and reinforces successful behavior.

- *Be prepared to do.* "Just a heads-up for you that Henny will be going to the conference next week, so your people will need to cover her desk till Thursday." This statement is about the future. After all, who wants to be caught unprepared by surprises?

Distinguish between the person and the behavior and the performance.

—Stephen Covey

What Planning Looks Like

When you look back at your three-step planning process for the 20-Minute Coaching Conversation, your expectation and feedback preparation might look like this:

- *Step 1: Identify.* "I would like you to spend a little more time reviewing our three-phrase customer call system with your team. The reason for this is that I have received a lot of questions from Marketing on what our call system is. We need to make sure that everyone experiences the system in the same way. If they don't, then people will make up their own responses, and we won't be consistent." Here you help the employee focus on the issue at hand: the customer call system. Now the stated goal of the meeting is immediate and clear, and you can spend quality time delivering feedback.

- *Step 2: Involve.* "What are your thoughts? What can we do to reinforce the customer care system?" Here you are actively involving the team member and opening up the floor to guided suggestions. Remember to participate in this phase of the conversation by prodding, suggesting, and guiding the conversation productively rather than inviting a rant about why "such and such team member isn't contributing" or "I just don't have the resources." Since they're not used to it, employees can often see this opportunity as merely a chance to vent, but that's not what it's for. Involve the employees, yes, but guide them as well.

- *Step 3: Initiate.* "I like your suggestion of holding a brief 15-minute meeting once a week to review the system with your team. I can also suggest that you ask some of our internal customers how they see the system working. Let's talk about this again in two weeks to check progress." Here is where you initiate some plan of action for the employee to take—in this case, a weekly meeting for system review and an evaluation by those all-important internal customers. You can also set up a follow-up meeting to make it clear to the employee that you're taking this action plan, and the feedback, seriously.

Don't forget that feedback can also be totally positive and fall into the same vein as "keep doing this." How would that look? Let's see, for "identify," you would tell the employee *what is working well*. To "involve" him or her, you would want to discuss *how to make what they're doing even better*, and finally, to "initiate," you would make *suggestions for action to be taken*.

Remember, whether you're giving feedback on what they're doing right or rewarding them for doing wrong less often, your employees *need* this feedback in regular doses. These exercises will help you give it to them *regularly*, *accurately*, and in a *detailed* manner that keeps them doing rather than guessing.

Now Try This

Whom on your team do you owe some quick feedback to? The following exercise can be used in just a few minutes of conversation for a fast course correction or can be worked into your 20-Minute Coaching Conversation using the *identify*, *involve*, and *initiate* model:

1. Do more of this:

    _____

2. Do less of this:

    _____

3. Keep doing this:

    _____

4. Be prepared to do this:

Try again. Fail again. Fail better.

—Samuel Beckett

PART 2

THE 20-MINUTE
MOTIVATION
CONVERSATION

CHAPTER 4

MOTIVATION MATTERS

Robert was enjoying his first day at his new job. And why not? After all, this was a day he'd been waiting for for quite some time. After bouncing around at two start-ups that had gone nowhere, here he was at a medium-sized Internet retailer, a solid, successful company, a place where he could finally put down some roots and make his home. Robert planned on staying here for a long time. So while he was sitting in the coffee room finishing some first-day paperwork, he was glad to see Bill, a longtime employee, come in for his coffee break.

"You're new, right?" said Bill over his shoulder as he poured himself a cup of coffee from the community machine.

"Yeah, been here all of five hours!" replied Robert, looking up from his W-2 forms.

"Welcome," Bill said cordially, offering his hand. "So, what brought you here?"

"I guess I got tired of playing musical chairs in my two previous start-up companies," Robert admitted truthfully.

"Well you won't find much different here," Bill told him. "We might as well be a start-up."

While Robert nearly dropped his pen, Bill continued his litany of complaints: "Management really messed up here," he insisted before continuing. "You can't really get anything done—and don't count on any support from your manager; they don't come with any backbone at all!"

Robert sat there dumbfounded. He had just met his first seriously disengaged coworker, but it would not be his last!

Robert reported this incident to me after we met at an industry conference recently. He told me that he never forgot that conversation with Bill. In fact, it colored his view of company management for many months to come. And it wasn't until he developed a trusting relationship with his current boss— "a really good boss," he said—that he was able to feel motivated and fully engaged in his work.

Robert's story shows the real-life dangers of workers who feel disengaged, out of the loop, neglected, and unappreciated. Like an infection, their disengagement spreads quickly, and it is only those who actively seek out the vaccine of engagement who can conquer this seemingly insurmountable sense of workplace ennui. While Robert was hearty enough to stick around and see for himself, many lesser employees might have run for cover after their break room meeting with Bill.

Which leads me to ask the seminal question, "What is this thing called 'engagement'?" According to the Conference

Board's 2008 report on Employee Engagement (a definition based on research over the past 10 years), it goes something like this: "Employee engagement is a heightened emotional and intellectual connection that an employee has for their job, organization, manager, or coworkers, that allows them to apply additional discretionary effort to their work."

Sounds about right to me. But let's examine the key phrases here, which are:

- "Emotional and intellectual connection"
- "To job, organization, manager and coworkers"
- "To apply additional discretionary effort"

If you think about it, this is more than a definition—it's really a formula for a motivated workforce. Leaders who understand these concepts and are able to operationalize their efforts to engage and motivate their employees have a profound effect on productivity throughout the organization.

Gallup employee polls have estimated the following percentages for employee engagement:

- Actively disengaged: 19 percent
- Disengaged: 23 percent

Let's just say that in Robert's encounter with Bill, he was dealing with an "actively disengaged" employee. But whether they're actively disengaged or just disengaged, how many "Bills" does it take to destroy the trust and productivity of a team? Just one. The Corporate Leadership Council (2004) found that highly engaged employees were 87 percent less likely to leave their companies than their disengaged counterparts.

The 20-Minute Motivating Conversation is an important part of the engagement puzzle. By acting as the "vaccine" to actively break the cycle of disengagement in your company, a department, or an employee, you not only immediately engage that employee but create in him or her a feeling of engagement that can help foster performance and increase satisfaction. In fact, a study by Towers Perrin (2005) identified these top drivers that inspire employees to engage and stay with their companies:

- A leader who connects
- Opportunities to grow in one's career
- A leader who is inspirational and enthusiastic
- A good reputation and pride in the company

The 20-Minute Motivating Conversation establishes you as an "all of the above" kind of leader; one who establishes, personifies, and lives these four qualities for the benefit of all employees, departmentwide and companywide. I believe you will find this conversation to be one of the most effective means possible of helping to engage employees on a daily basis.

Other studies confirm that motivated and engaged employees add heavily to the bottom-line success of an organization, and over and over again we find research that reveals that having "a personal relationship with one's manager"—a relationship in which employees feel that the leader cares about their career growth—works toward employee satisfaction on the job.

If you can't change your fate, change your attitude.

—Amy Tan

Intrinsic versus Extrinsic Motivation

When people feel motivated, they are engaged and interested in their work. Think about the last time you were fully involved in an activity and time just flew by; you were not watching the clock, but instead were totally absorbed in the pure joy of the work or the task. That's motivation, and it's what all leaders want from their team members.

In this chapter, we will look at something called *intrinsic motivation*, which comes from the work itself. We are not talking about money or promotion, which is considered *extrinsic motivation*. Extrinsic motivation, such as pay and/or promotion, is not something that managers have much control over—certainly not enough to use it to engage and motivate others.

Think about the last time you got a pay raise. How much harder did you work?

Probably not much, but why? Because you felt that *the company owed you that raise*. And, if the company owed you that money, it felt more like back pay, not a motivational factor that would get you to work harder than you were already working. Such mindsets are part and parcel of the modern workforce; wrong or right, they must be dealt with realistically to create and foster engagement. If money isn't enough, we must understand what *is* enough—and give it to them.

Research tells us that money is important. We need it to live and manage our lives and care for our families. But unless it's a wheelbarrow full of money—in other words, a lifestyle-changing amount of money—it does not engage or motivate us for very long. In any event, however, the pay must be regarded as fair.

Intrinsic motivation, consisting of factors that come from the work itself, is what engages employees the most. We will explore key questions and leadership behaviors that help give people energy, passion, and meaningful work. One of the important behaviors used in this 20-Minute Conversation is making appropriate suggestions based on the needs of the individual. In other words, to suggest is to make clear recommendations that are relevant to the situation.

People make suggestions all the time. Too often, these suggestions are lost in the discussion or simply ignored by others. This is particularly true if you're trying to influence a highly active meeting.

What You Think versus What Employees Want

When you engage your employees, you need to do more than merely consider extrinsic versus intrinsic factors. What about the difference between what you think employees want and what they really want? You might be surprised at the vast gulf between expectation and reality. In our research, when we ask managers what they think motivates their employees, they say the following two things, in this order:

- First, 88 percent say it's *money*.
- Second, 67 percent say it's *promotion*.

And, of course, these are the most obvious and the easiest answers, because they are largely outside of the control of most leaders. "What can we do?" they say. "There is just so much money and promotion to go around." And, of course, they are right. Both of these categories are outside motivators, or what we call extrinsic motivation.

When we ask employees what motivates them, however, they say that two things, primarily, motivate them—in this order:

- First, 76 percent say it's interesting and *meaningful work*.
- Second, 72 percent say it's *new learning* and *professional growth*.

These, of course, are intrinsic motivators, and they're what we'll be concentrating on in this chapter. When it comes to extrinsic versus intrinsic motivation, there seems to be a gap between what leaders believe and what employees really want in order to feel more engaged, loyal, and motivated. This is a very dangerous gap, because ignoring these quick, focused conversations that go far toward energizing, motivating, and retaining the talent they need now and into the future costs companies big dollars.

According to the ISR Corporation in Chicago, new data suggest a 52 percent difference in one-year performance improvement in operating income between companies with highly engaged employees compared to companies with low engagement, a 13 percent improvement in net income growth over a one-year period at companies with high employee engagement, and a 28 percent improvement in earnings per share growth at companies with high employee engagement. Clearly, such findings make an extreme case for the importance of intrinsic motivators to modern employees.

So, yes, leaders are eager to begin these conversations, but we find that before they try to motivate others, leaders need to make sure that they are feeling motivated and engaged themselves. Why? Because if you're running on empty—if you're no longer motivated yourself—it's going to be darn hard for you to engage your workforce with honesty and integrity.

Employees need to trust that their leaders are honest—that what they're saying isn't just a flavor of the month that they learned at some management seminar. In fact, we want leaders to really mean what they say and ask real questions that they really want to hear the answers to. And, yes, that they are not just using some technique but really care about the well-being and job satisfaction of their employees.

Before they try to motivate others, leaders need to take the Motivational Engagement Survey themselves to find out how much they know about their own engagement needs.

What Matters Most?

Many people get involved in their work and daily lives and forget what it is that really makes work worthwhile. By paying attention to what really matters, you can take responsibility for recharging yourself regardless of the circumstances. Some people seem to have the gift of bringing out the best in others. And other people falter when it comes to the finer points of motivation. What accounts for the difference?

Leaders who are skilled at motivation aren't magicians. They're simply adept at asking questions, listening carefully—and then doing something with what they've learned. Manipulation and motivation are not the same. One of the key differentiators is that of intent: manipulators set out to achieve their goals by promising, cajoling, and badgering others based on perceived hot buttons.

A motivator's intent is to bring out the best in others, and to do that by genuinely understanding what is important to others. A motivator creates a work environment that matches employees' key needs and standards. The tool introduced in this chapter is your starting point for understanding yourself and leading others.

Nothing great was ever achieved without enthusiasm.

—Ralph Waldo Emerson

Take This Motivational Engagement Survey

Read through the following list of motivational factors. Circle the *seven motivating factors* that have the most meaning to you, then categorize them in the exercise that follows the list.

1. Feeling a sense of personal involvement
2. Being recognized for doing good work
3. Being seen as very competent
4. Choosing my own projects and priorities
5. Getting meaningful feedback
6. Being my own boss
7. Experiencing a personal sense of challenge
8. Feeling respected by others
9. Having a sense of independence
10. Having a clear vision for future development
11. Working with people who care about one another
12. Having career plans and goals
13. Being part of group loyalty and security
14. Learning something new and satisfying
15. Working alone, self-managed
16. Working with a great team
17. Feeling accomplished
18. Working for the greater good
19. Setting my own standards and goals
20. Working for a good cause
21. Working for the best organization
22. Having the freedom to create and innovate

23. Working for a great boss
24. Doing exciting work that makes a contribution or impact

Four A's That Motivate

Write the key words for your seven most motivating choices from the previous list next to the corresponding numbers that follow. Then circle the numbers that correspond to the *two* most important motivating choices right now in your work life. Being aware of all seven is important, but focusing on the top two is very important right now.

What is your personal profile telling you?

Autonomy

The employee who is in search of *autonomy* is seeking choice and control, prefers work that allows for independent thought and action, and sets and follows personal standards regardless of the environment.

4. _____   16. _____
7. _____   20. _____
11. _____   24. _____

These 24 items are part of a larger survey, *Vengel Motivation-Engagement Survey*, used in our Three Leadership Conversations training program.

Achievement

Someone who wants *achievement* seeks performance and competence, prefers work that leads to tangible results, is comfortable with challenges, and is oriented toward goal setting and goal accomplishment.

2. _____   10. _____
3. _____   17. _____
8. _____   22. _____

Affiliation

The employee who is in search of *affiliation* seeks community and camaraderie; prefers work that fosters teamwork, relationships, and mentoring; and is interested in achieving results with and through others.

1. _____   15. _____
5. _____   18. _____
9. _____   21. _____

Actualization

The employee who is bent on *actualization* seeks purpose and principles; prefers work that aligns or integrates with a greater purpose, whether that purpose is personal, organizational, or spiritual; and seeks work that holds personal meaning.

6. _____   14. _____
12. _____   19. _____
13. _____   23. _____

What you have just done with this exercise is taken a big step toward defining who you are when it comes to your own engagement at work. And as we said earlier, as a leader, you must be aware of and be able to satisfy what you need in order to stay engaged.

How will you get closer to your engagement and motivational needs? Well, for starters, check out the following tips. They will offer you clues to what you need and clues to what your talented employees will be needing.

For example, if your two most important motivation factors were both under the autonomy heading or if you have an employee whose two most important factors are in autonomy, then you will have a great place to start your 20-Minute Motivating Conversation.

Now Try These Quick Tips

Use these practical ideas to boost your ability to motivate others. Circle two or three tips that may help you increase your awareness and flexibility and help you have the 20-Minute Motivation Conversation with an employee.

Motivating Autonomy Seekers

- Whenever you can, delegate as much as possible.
- Provide authority for projects along with the responsibility.
- Don't micromanage them.
- Ask for their recommendations and ideas.
- Don't force them to go along with the crowd if it's not necessary.

- Respect their independence.
- Be generous with responsibility.

Motivating Achievement Seekers

- Keep them up to date on their progress.
- Give them improvement-oriented feedback.
- Make their accomplishments visible.
- Work with them to set challenging goals.
- Fill them in on the big picture.
- Respect their need to know the plan, and share information with them.
- Be generous with praise and recognition.

Motivating Affiliation Seekers

- Share your networks.
- Mentor them or help them to find mentors.
- Include them in group projects.
- Appreciate their ability to initiate relationships and activities.
- Use them to build connections with key people and departments.
- Take part in activities with them.
- Be generous with your attention.

Motivating Actualization Seekers

- Listen carefully when they have concerns.
- Help them connect their work to their life goals.
- Respect their personal convictions.
- Ask how their values are being met at work.
- Respect their need to do significant work.
- Give them time to think and reflect.
- Be generous with your respect.

Leadership Action Plan

Imagine that the people who work for you don't need their paychecks, benefits, or perks. Imagine that they come to work each day as volunteers because they genuinely want to. If that were the case, what would they find motivating enough about your leadership to bring them in the door each day?

The job market may boom and bust, yet most people report that factors beyond steady pay and benefits are what keep them coming to work and giving their best. Use this action plan to build your capabilities as a motivational manager.

As a leader, your challenge is to be able to motivate in any of the four areas, if that's what your people need. What is most important to you as a leader in the following four areas? Do a quick summary for yourself:

- Autonomy_____
- Achievement_____
- Affiliation_____
- Actualization_____

Using the quick tips for leaders in the previous section, now think about one of your key employees, someone whom you want to know more about, a person who you believe needs engagement and a 20-Minute Motivating Conversation. To prepare, you may have this person take a quick survey on the Web site www.Vengelconsulting.com or you can take a guess about what might be important to them about the four areas.

Which two areas will be most important to your employee?

If one of these areas is *autonomy*, what questions do you want to ask?

_____

If one of them is *achievement*, what questions do you want to ask?

_____

If one of them is *affiliation*, what questions do you want to ask?

_____

If one of them is *actualization*, what questions do you want to ask?

The most important thing to get out of this exercise—and this chapter—is a better understanding of *what makes you tick* and a willingness to understand more about *what makes your people tick*.

You will find that there are some similarities and some important differences. Not everyone is engaged and motivated by exactly the same things. Understanding this and being able to do something worthwhile, to actually take some action on behalf of your employees, is what separates great leaders from the ordinary.

And it's going to take only 20 minutes!

Most people live and die with their music still unplayed. They never dare to try.

—Mary Kay Ash

CHAPTER 5

FOCUS AND MAKE THE CONVERSATIONS REAL

It was Year-End Bonus Day, and you could hear a pin drop in the company auditorium. The VP who was spelling out the company's success and future plans had what looked like every employee spellbound. Except for one, that is; her name was Sarah, and while the rest of the company was busy making plans for the next fiscal year, Sarah was busy putting her résumé together. Earlier in the day, the very same VP who had the company spellbound had distributed the year-end bonuses—and Sarah's was a big one.

Twelve months ago, Sarah had been offered a unique challenge: rolling out a new IT system worldwide. Naturally, with great responsibility comes great sacrifice, and this was no exception; it would require plenty of sacrifice on her part (namely, putting her family and friends on hold for a year while she traveled the globe), but the reward would be worth it: a huge year-end bonus more than equal to her yearly salary. *So*, she decided, *yes, she would do it!* And she did; she put 100 percent of her time and effort into the project's success.

Missing her son's third birthday and her older daughter's soccer match was simply part of the bargain. Saving the company millions of dollars was the goal, and she reached it, but at a cost to her personal life, as her friends and family were constantly wondering where she was. And now, as she recounted the story to me, the "big day for the big payoff" had finally arrived—the VP from the home office back east had flown into town with the bonus checks.

Sarah was still fuming as she began her story. "He came into my office with the envelope in hand and, almost throwing it on my desk, said, 'I guess this one is yours,' then just walked out. I sat there—without moving—for a few minutes. I remember thinking, 'I can't believe the way he just threw that money at me!'"

"What did you do next?" I prodded, eager to hear more— and secretly hoping that the VP had merely been joking or, if not, had found a way to rebound from his critical blunder.

"My first impulse was to follow him out the door and just rip that check up in his face!"

"What did you do instead?" I asked.

"I cashed it, of course! But the minute I did, I said, 'I'm out of here!' That guy didn't even say thank you, not a shred of appreciation or recognition of what I went through for the company—that's the way my boss, Jeff, is too. And I'm worth more than that. I said, 'I'm putting my résumé together now,' and that's exactly what I did."

(Don't Just) Show Me the Money!

Unfortunately, Sarah's story is not unique. Leaders make lots of assumptions about their people, and many of them truly believe that it's really just about money. For these leaders, it's not how the money is delivered, how it's positioned, or, for that matter, how it's earned; they use money as their sole reward, and the rest is just so many minor details.

For Sarah, however, the bonus was only part of her motivation; the other (perhaps bigger) part of her motivation and engagement in the project was the challenge and the acknowledgment of a job well done. Jeff, her immediate boss, obviously did not really know Sarah, let alone understand what motivated and engaged her to go the extra step needed for success. And if Jeff didn't know Sarah, how could the VP from the home office back east possibly hope to know her?

What could Jeff have done not only to ensure the completion of a successful global project, but also to retain a valuable and dedicated employee? For starters, he could have invested 20 minutes to engage Sarah in a motivational conversation. And if he wasn't up to the task, the VP in question should have taken the time instead.

Here is yet another reason why 20 minutes is such an effective number—and how being able to replicate it anytime, anywhere can possibly gain you thousands of minutes of effective employee conduct in the bargain.

Sarah was not just another employee; here was someone who was willing and able to dedicate a year of her life to rolling out a new IT system worldwide. Even if you have no idea how this task might be accomplished, you can probably guess that accomplishing it is a task in and of itself! Yet Sarah was not only up for the task, but up for the challenge. She was clearly looking to impress, to make a name for herself, and to provide for the company and her own security, and, yes, she was willing to sacrifice in return for a hefty year-end bonus.

Well, Sarah got the bonus, but nothing else. Not an "atta girl," not a pat on the back, not even a glancing nod of recognition. Did Sarah protest? Did she stick around and ask to talk to Jeff or the VP or someone else at the home office? Did she state her opinion or provide answers for an exit interview or in any other way voice her concerns? No, and why should she? The onus of engagement is not solely on the employee; it's principally on you, the leader.

Now Jeff will have to find someone else with just as much initiative, talent, and motivation (good luck!), and the VP will be counting on Jeff to do so, and quickly. Jeff could have solved his and the VP's problem with 20 simple minutes, yet he didn't. And Sarah walked, free and clear.

And who could blame her?

How—and Why—to Engage Employees

Getting to know your talented people at a deeper level is paramount for having an engaged workforce. As we have seen, the cost of *not* getting to know folks can be measured in more than merely dollars and cents.

According to authors Beverly Kaye and Sharon Jordan-Evans, who wrote the book *Love 'Em or Lose 'Em: Getting Good*

People to Stay (Berrett-Koehler Publishers, 2008), it's more than pay that engages and retains the best people. They've asked more than 20,000 people what keeps them and engages them in their organization, and, once again, the top three answers are

1. Career growth and challenge
2. Exciting work
3. Great people

Money doesn't even make the top-three list! And the authors go on to say that managers really don't know their people well because they don't just fail to find out what's really important to people—they don't even ask! An important part of the 20-Minute Motivation Conversation is asking.

No two of your people will have the same exact answer to the question, "What is most important to your motivation and engagement in the company?" However, if you have the opportunity to run your team through a Motivational Engagement Survey, that will help. If you don't, you still can begin this important conversation with some specific questions and planning.

So why guess? Why not ask your people what's most important?

In my research, I have found that there are four main reasons why leaders don't ask:

1. "We don't have time."
2. "We can't do anything about it anyway."
3. "We'll set up an expectation that we won't be able to fulfill, and people will be disappointed."

4. "We don't know how. It's awkward for us to start such a conversation."

Four Reasons Why Leaders Don't Ask

These are obviously very real and valid concerns, as they keep coming up over and over again—the same four concerns, consistently. So let's take care of this right now. How do we address these concerns? *Here* is how we address them.

Reason 1: "We Don't Have Time"

What kind of time are we talking about? 60 minutes? 45 minutes? 30 minutes? No, just 20 minutes. Don't you have even that much time to spare to engage, motivate, and foster results in talented people?

According to Bliss & Associates, an "advisory service to cultivate exceptional leadership," the cost of hiring and training a new employee is considerably more than what that employee is paid per year. Specifically, "These calculations will easily reach 150% of the employees' annual compensation figure. The cost will be significantly higher (200% to 250% of annual compensation) for managerial and sales positions."

Now do you have 20 minutes? Sure you do.

Every one of the leaders we've talked with agrees that he or she has 20 minutes—especially when the leader is faced with the downside repercussions of a disengaged workforce and retaining key talent for the future. The time and effort required to reengage employees and to replace good employees, not to mention the obvious associated costs, is far more intensive then preventive measures such as having your 20-Minute Conversations ahead of the curve.

Reason 2: "We Can't Do Anything about It Anyway"

Well, how do you know that unless you ask people? Again, most of the leaders we talked with believe that it's money or promotion that keeps employees on board, fat and happy—and those things are limited—but there is a great deal that leaders can do for employees when they learn about the more intrinsic motivation that people are craving.

Consider the things that really matter to your people. You can either use the three-item list given in this chapter—career growth and challenge, exciting work, and great people—or develop one after a few 20-Minute Conversations of your own. Aren't these things that you *can* control? Don't they come in unlimited quantities?

Once managers see that they do have some control over these motivators—interesting work, and career growth and challenge—they feel more empowered and resourceful in meeting employees' engagement needs as well as their own.

Reason 3: "We'll Set Up Expectations That We Won't Be Able to Fulfill"

No one wants to disappoint employees by promising what he cannot deliver.

But what employee wants a boss who never even tries? Or who never even asks the questions—or has never taken the 20 minutes to explore the engagement issues? Employees want honest conversations with managers who have the courage to ask the right questions and then at least listen and discuss possibilities for 20 minutes.

Reason 4: "We Don't Know How"

Well, of course you don't. At least, not unless you were lucky enough to have a boss in your past who knew what real leadership was—and who actually talked with you about your goals and your motivation at work.

Most people learn from what they see around them and what others have done with them, and if you have never seen it or experienced it, you would not really know how to have a quick, efficient, focused conversation on motivational factors with each of your people. Now let's see what this conversation looks like and sounds like.

What are the behaviors that you will use?

The Seven Behaviors of the 20-Minute Motivation Conversation

If the motivational conversation is to be successful, your focus as a leader must be on the other person and on what is most interesting and engaging to that person. It is the ultimate "walk a mile in their moccasins" moment, and to get the most out of this meeting, the behaviors that you will be using will be primarily Pull in nature.

In other words, rather than Pushing the issue that most concerns you, you will instead be inviting the other person to contribute to the conversation. As a result, the employee will be adding to the body of data about him- or herself and helping you decide how best to use that employee.

In many cases, it will be the first time that any manager has really asked employees these types of questions—questions that will help them to unleash their energy and passion in the work they do.

The seven behaviors of the 20-Minute Motivation Conversation will look like this.

Behavior 1: Ask Open-Ended Questions

These are questions that do not have a yes or no answer, but instead require more content and explanation by the employee. For instance, open-ended questions frequently sound like this:

- "What are your interests?"
- "What excites you about the work?"
- "What part of your work is most meaningful?"

These are great Pull questions. They allow the employee to answer in any area in which he or she has experience.

Behavior 2: Ask Focused Questions

Focused questions will help you drill down for deeper understanding:

- "Which of the things we've talked about is most interesting to you?"
- "Would you tell me more about the best project you've
worked on?"
- "Which of these tasks matches your goals?"

Behavior 3: Summarize

"Summarizing" behavior allows you to repeat back to the
employee what you're hearing and understanding, bringing
clarity for both of you. Remember, summarizing what the
employee has just said to you provides evidence that you have
not only heard what she is saying but also understand what she
has just said. It's the most important listening behavior, and it
often sounds like this:

- "So what you're saying is this: . . ."
- "Here is what I am hearing about your interests."
- "It sounds like you really like to complete projects from
A to Z."

Behavior 4: Create a Vision

What does success look like? What is a picture of the employee
working in an engaged state? Visualizing this behavior lets the

employee know that you have a sense of what the future can be like for him or her:

- "Here's what I see for you."
- "The picture I have is for you to be working more like this: . . ."

Behavior 5: Provide a Rationale

These are your reasons why the employee should help to create more engagement. It helps to build a case for doing something differently—after all, you are going to want to move the employee to action.

- "Some reasons I think you might enjoy working in this area are . . ."
- "Based on what you've said, here is a rationale that supports your new learning: . . ."

Behavior 6: Disclose

This behavior is important for establishing trust and letting the employee know your motives for having this conversation. It also allows you to share what engages you in the present and has engaged you in the past.

- "Some of the factors that motivate me are similar to yours: . . ."

- "There have been times in the past when I have felt stuck, and here is what I did: . . ."
- "I'm not sure what we can do right now, but let's be creative . . ."

Behavior 7: Suggest

This will be your call to action. The 20-Minute Motivation Conversation will need to end with some movement or next step. Without this, the conversation might seem pointless, without a clear direction in which to follow up.

- "My recommendation is that you look at this task a little differently . . ."
- "Perhaps we should try this new idea for two weeks . . ."
- "My idea is that we think about this point for a couple of days, then meet again . . ."

These are behaviors that I would recommend; the order in which you use them may change and is, of course, flexible. But we find that starting with Pull questions and energy is most important. And, of course, you can circle back into the listening behaviors frequently during your time frame.

A typical Motivation Conversation between Hal (the manager) and Karen (the employee) might sound like this:

Hal: I'm glad that we've found a few minutes to have a conversation. I know things have been moving pretty quickly around here.

Karen: Yeah, I rarely have time to catch my breath. It seems like we're always jumping to new things.

Hal: I'd like to find out how you're seeing your work, and maybe how we can make it more interesting for you. What are some of the more interesting things you are doing?

Karen: "Well, a lot of it's interesting, like the detailed analysis I got to do with Ted's team. But sometimes I don't get a sense of completion. As I said, we keep on jumping to the new thing.

Hal: Sounds like the "new thing" is getting in the way of some of your enjoyment.

Karen: Well, the new thing is exciting at times, and I know you need me to be able to get the next project started; it just feels as if I just get my teeth into something, then someone else takes over.

Hal: "What would make the work more satisfying for you? It sounds as if you want to stay with a project longer.

Karen: I think that's it. I want my fingerprints on a project, something that I can point to and say that it was something I accomplished.

Hal: You said earlier that the analysis you did for Ted's team was interesting. What was it about that that made you feel good?

Karen: I got to do something and present it to the whole team at that big meeting we had. I felt like it was mine, my contribution to a successful project.

Hal: I have an idea. Why don't we look for more ways to carve out chunks of a project that you can call your own? I'll still need you to do some jumping around to help me get new projects started, but at least you will get a sense that you've had the accomplishments you're seeking, and we can work in a couple of presentations to upper management on what you're doing. How does that sound?"

Never Let Vanilla Be Your "Flavor of the Month"

This example would be a great beginning to this 20-Minute Motivation Conversation. Better yet, it would give both Karen and Hal something to think about for the next meeting—and there *will* be a next meeting, whether it is a week, two weeks or even a month from now. Or, at least, there should be if all of this is to be effective.

No one likes to be part of the latest "leadership fad" or to simply go through the motions because the boss comes back all excited after that big training seminar in DC. Employees become particularly savvy about the whims and fleeting fancies of their leaders, even if you haven't yet.

If such conversations are to be successful in the long term (and why else would you have them?), both parties must be confident that this is not a one-time pep talk, not a singular "event," but rather how we will do business together regularly to ensure that *all* needs are met: the leader's, the employee's, *and* the organization's.

To make sure that you and your employees make a habit of the 20-Minute Motivation Conversation, remember these five engagement-motivational tips:

1. *Stay focused on issues that are within each person's control.* Be creative; find what is controllable, and make those things a priority rather than focusing on some "pie-in-the-sky" goal that neither of you can realistically achieve.

2. *Stay positive, but realistic.* You don't need to be Pollyanna; just acknowledge what is not possible or is not working now and focus on what can work soon.

3. *Look at the bigger picture first.* Show perspective by presenting the long-term, big-picture scenario, then move down to a doable action step to move you both toward that ultimate goal.

4. *Stay away from false promises.* Pie-in-the-sky pay raises or promotions in the future may lead to disappointments when they don't materialize or measure up. Focus on what you can do realistically; your sincerity in trying to make a difference is important both now and in the future.

5. *Stay on track with what is best for this individual.* Staying on track means rescheduling when you cannot make a meeting or checking in on how the process is going before and after the meeting. This will help the employee to realize that this 20-Minute Conversation was important to you—not just another "flavor of the month."

Speaking of "flavor of the month," this is a phrase that is commonly used by most managers and employees to describe a new way of doing business. What it really means, of course, is that this new method won't last!

After all, flavors of the month are designed to go away once the month is over, or at least to cease being special. I mean, who still wants to taste December's Peppermint Patty Mocha by the end of January or as spring begins? When you introduce something as "the flavor of the month," either intentionally or simply with uninterested or unrealistic phrasing or body language, your employees will know that you're not serious about it.

Case in point: Pete sat in my training program for most of the day with a cynical look on his face, but didn't speak up until the last hour we had together.

"This is just the latest 'flavor of the month,' isn't it?" he finally asked. "Every year or so the leadership group decides to run a new one on us," he went on to explain. "So this year it's the 20-Minute Conversation engagement thing."

"What are you really looking for from this approach, Pete?" I asked him. "What do you really want? Because it sounds like you've seen it all, right?"

"Yeah, I have in the 15 years I've been a manager here, I really have, and it all sounds good. I guess what I really want is for it to be real. Not just another idea that comes and goes with no follow-up or measuring. And I would like to see my boss have this conversation with me! *That* would be real."

Well, no one can argue with that. We all want these conversations, and we want them to be meaningful for ourselves and for our employees. What we don't want is to do this once—and then never again. That not only defeats the purpose of these 20-Minute Conversations, but also undermines our potential for leadership.

There's nothing wrong with introducing something new and phasing it out if it doesn't work; that's called trial and error, and it's what most companies in this country do every day. But to try something new once and then lose interest, passion, or motivation before giving it a chance to work is doubly frustrating—for you and for your employees.

So go ahead, introduce the 20-Minute Motivation Conversation as your "flavor of the month," because this system really works, and if you do it right and do it often, your employees will develop a taste for it right off the bat!

And what about you? What's your favorite flavor—or style—of leadership? Later in this book, we will revisit what leaders need for themselves around these three conversations, because if they are running on empty, it's real hard to fill up anyone else's tank. Right now, though, let's take a quick look at a five-minute plan to help you prepare for your 20-Minute Motivation Conversation:

Step 1: Identify

Identify the specific issues that you want to address during the conversation:

- *Be clear about what motivates and engages this person.* "I want to understand what engages you most in your work."

- *Ask open-ended questions.* "What do you find most satisfying? How about least satisfying?"
- *Ask focused questions.* "You've told me about three or four things—what is at the top of your list right now?"

Step 2: Involve

In this step, focus more deeply on this person's motivational priorities, using the following tools:

- *Summarize.* "So, what you're most interested in is this: . . . ?"
- *Create a vision.* "What I can see in the future is this possibility: . . ."
- *Disclose.* "I'm not sure what we can do now, but here is some of my experience: . . ."
- *Provide a rationale.* "These are my two reasons for saying this: . . ."

Step 3: Initiate

Concentrate on the next steps you'll need to take to move forward by using these two types of questions:

- *Suggest.* "Let me put this idea out there for you . . ."
- *Ask focused questions.* "Is this something that you can commit to for the next two weeks?"

Remember that the conversation will not follow these exact examples, of course, but by preparing in advance, you will be ready and can adjust to what is needed to conduct and manage these 20 minutes to a positive conclusion.

Now You Try It

Just fill in these three steps for your next 20-Minute Motivation Conversation.

Step 1: Identify

_____

_____

Step 2: Involve

_____

_____

Step 3: Initiate

_____

_____

CHAPTER **6**

HOW TO ENGAGE EMPLOYEES THROUGH MOTIVATION

I was told this story recently by a senior director at a very successful Internet company:

> *Todd had many important competencies, valuable skills that my team needed. Unfortunately, he showed them only on those rare occasions when he rose to his full potential; most of the time Todd did his job quietly but . . . barely.*
>
> *We had spoken often about this seeming contradiction, or gulf, between what he could be and what he actually contributed. We even did some coaching, but nothing seemed to light his fire or ignite his passion for the work, for the team, or, for that matter, for me. Every once in a while he would show a flash of brilliance that would startle me into realizing his true potential—only to have it disappear a week later into his default setting of mediocrity.*

I had tried to have a motivating conversation with him, even though it was new to me and I was very awkward with my end of the conversation. Not surprisingly, Todd was somewhat put off by my attempt to engage him in this talk, and it didn't go as either one of us had planned. I even heard him tell a coworker that it sounded like "HR mumbo jumbo."

I went back to my office feeling as if I had just stepped into a Dilbert cartoon.

I spoke with my boss about Todd, and about my failed attempts to bring out his passion; she told me that it sounded as if I was doing my best and that "you can lead a horse to water, but you can't make him drink."

She added, "Not everyone will be able to—or even wants to—go to the next level of performance." And she said that perhaps Todd would "come around" in his own time. Her final verdict was that "we must let it ride." After all, Todd was performing—just not at the level that he was capable of.

Then, a couple of months later, Bam! A flash of brilliance: Todd had taken a project that should have taken eight weeks to complete and had done it in five weeks!

"How did you do that, Todd?" I asked him.

"Well,' he explained, 'before I dove into the project, I did a little research and found a similar project that another team had done a couple of years ago—so instead of having to start from zero and building something new, I could bolt the new parts we needed onto the basic

foundation." As he related all this to me, his eyes grew bright and excited; it was an expression of true passion and total engagement.

"Sounds like this is really something you like to do," I said.

"Yeah, I guess so. It's kind of like a challenge, like solving a mystery."

"What if we could engineer some of your time to focus on other projects in the same way—would that be interesting?"

"Cool," was all he said.

During the next year, Todd did three more projects in half the time that we had scoped for them. One project he advised us to scrap altogether, showing the team how it was unnecessary and not well designed, and, in the process, saving the company many thousands of dollars and team energy.

So that's what full engagement can do, I thought as I ruminated on the way Todd had seemed to be reborn in his enthusiasm and passion for work—once we found a way to get, and keep, him motivated.

Todd's turnaround taught me a lot about patience, about not accepting the status quo, and about putting people on projects that allowed them to use the best of their abilities. I also learned not to give up, that sometimes you need to wait a bit and give employees a chance to think about your conversations and then circle back around.

20 Minutes for the Conversation— Not the Results!

Remember, while these are 20-Minute Conversations, that doesn't necessarily mean that the results will come quite so quickly. Look at Todd; it took a few sit-downs to rein him in and get him back on track with what he truly felt passionate and purposeful about.

We have to keep in mind that this is a process and that some employees will respond to these conversations more quickly than others. That's why I stress the need to make these conversations a habit rather than an event; one time simply wouldn't have been enough for someone like Todd, and look how great he ended up being once he got motivated enough to believe in himself, his abilities, his company, and, of course, his leader.

Leadership is a process, growth is a process, change is a process; if we rush these or any of the other 1,001 processes that contribute to business success, we run the risk of giving up too soon, too often, and missing out on the benefits that good employees offer once they are sufficiently motivated to perform to their potential.

You can be totally rational with a machine, but, if you work with people, sometimes logic has to take a backseat to understanding.

—Akio Morita

Practice "Active Patience"

While patience is a virtue, it is not our only one. Waiting around for inspiration to strike wouldn't have worked with Todd, and it won't work with most, if any, employees. It is human nature for us to become habitual about our performance; if we are continually praised, responded to, given and asked for feedback, and motivated, we will progress naturally. If we are habitually ignored, denied feedback, and taken for granted, we will do the bare minimum until we are called out for it.

So we must be patient, but we must also be active. These 20-Minute Motivation Conversations are all about something that I call "active patience." They are habits that we form to create productive employees through a series of conversations (not one single event) that we actively pursue as part of the bigger picture known as productivity.

Timing is the key to active patience; that is why patience is on an equal footing with action! If we rush results, we risk the backlash that comes from disaffected, insulted, harried, and unmotivated employees.

After all, motivation relies on various critical factors that must align to produce true employee passion. Sometimes the timing is not right; sometimes you are not at your best. Sometimes the right person is on the wrong project or the wrong person is on the right project; other times an employee is shoved into the wrong position or pushed out of the right one.

Or the employee may not be quite ready for more engagement, or may not be ready to be motivated in a way that you think she should be. But you know that this employee can be a top performer, and so you offer your hand, a hand of invitation in the form of a 20-Minute Motivation Conversation. And sometimes the employee does not take the invitation.

He or she ignores your hand. But you offer it again at another time—a week or a month later. Persistent "good will" that invites the employee to more satisfying, meaningful work is an important part of each leader's job. It is also at the foundation of "active patience."

Don't Be "Puzzled," Just Give Yourself Time to See the Big Picture

As we can see from the story that began this chapter, which was told to me by a senior director at a very successful Internet company, people are already motivated; they just need someone to tap into them personally. Over and above our needs, which are equally important, we must discover what is motivating and engaging to our employees. The goal then is to help direct this, focus it, and turn it into performance. And that's the leader's job.

These 20-Minute Performance-Oriented Conversations will take some skill, courage, and persistence, and a mind-set that never gives up. There will be no one answer to what gets people's passion and energy up, but rather multiple pieces that must gel and mesh for us to fully understand and successfully utilize them to get employees motivated, passionate, and sincere.

In a way, it's really like a puzzle; there are lots of pieces of relevant information that need to be put together before we, and the employee, can see the big picture. And sometimes, like Todd, even the employee does not know what the puzzle looks like.

Then a great manager comes along, one who is willing to look, offer, and invite the individual on an ongoing basis, and bingo, you have people and teams that really perform. That intersection between an able and willing employee and a patient and active leader is where true motivation comes from.

Six Essential Truths about Motivation and Engagement

Everyone wants the "secret" to motivation, but, as we saw with Todd, it's rare that one simple strategy or solution works for every employee. Rather, motivation is personal, nuanced, and unique to each employee. So instead of secrets, tips, tactics, or tricks, I offer instead the following six universal truths about motivation and engagement.

The First Truth: Engagement Is Individual and Personal

Stop looking outside for cookie-cutter answers and look inward for peace and solutions. The more you know about yourself and what keeps you motivated, the smarter you'll be about others. By understanding yourself as a leader, you will have clues for understanding your talented people.

You will also come to the realization that other people may not be motivated by the same things that you are. One big mistake that many managers make is to assume that of course everyone is engaged by the same things they are. Don't assume this! Really, not everyone is into achievement the way you may be. Perhaps other people get jazzed by the benefit of the greater good, by being a part of something bigger than themselves, by leaving a lasting legacy, or by sheer self-interest and promotion.

Don't see your role as influencer or changer as meaning that everyone must conform to what makes you motivated. Instead, through self-examination and active patience, work hard to understand what motivates others, and then use that knowledge to, in fact, motivate them.

The Second Truth: Motivation Is Not Manipulation

Many times people feel manipulated in a negative way by outside extrinsic rewards, such as money, tips, or trophies, but what *really* makes for manipulation is when someone has a hidden agenda—i.e., is not letting others know the truth.

The leaders we deal with who are the best at developing top performance are always clear and truthful about their motives; this really helps them to create success and bring out the best in people.

The Third Truth: Recognize Their Accomplishments

"No one recognized what I could do" is one of the top reasons that people cite for moving on or shutting down on the job. In fact, more people report disengaging and leaving a job because no one recognized their accomplishments than for nearly any other reason. Yet recognition is one of the simplest, quickest, and most effective forms of conversation to have with an employee.

Appreciation for a job well done is easy to give and is often priceless for the individual. Truly, it just takes a minute of your time—or sometimes just a quick 20-Minute Conversation that is planned and focused around the goal of motivation.

The Fourth Truth: Challenge, Challenge, Challenge

Many of the respondents to our five-year survey of leaders reported hearing the following two phrases more often than not: "I want to learn something new once in a while" and "I want to see my contribution mean something."

When we asked the groups of employees participating in our questionnaires what was most important to them when they were considering new jobs, they overwhelmingly said—to the tune of 83 percent of respondents—that it was challenge on the job and meaningful contributions at the workplace.

Clearly, if employees are to feel motivated, we must keep their jobs interesting. We all come to the workplace every day, park in the same spot, ride the same elevator, and sit in the same cubicle or office. A little challenge from time to time goes a long way. In this case, challenge can come in the form of the opportunity to perform at a new level. Remember, the challenge does not have to be big—just different, small, and significant at times.

The Fifth Truth: Ownership

"What have I done that I can point to and say that it's mine?"

This is a common refrain heard from employees in and out of our hundreds of seminars. People want to have an impact on the big picture and to know that their work made a difference, and if they can't see this, then it takes a good boss to point it out to them—clearly and with real appreciation.

Like recognition, appreciation is truly free; a kind and specific word about a recent achievement, a significant contribution, or even just a bright idea can often mean the difference between motivation and mediocrity.

The Sixth Truth: Involvement

"Get me involved in some decision," employees are saying more and more often. "I want to be part of the process." When people are involved in the process, they are more likely to be committed to the results, and what leader wouldn't give his eyeteeth for real commitment from his team?

The best part about involvement is that it feeds into and unto itself. Once an employee begins to feel involved in his or her department, in his or her team, or even in conversations with you, the snowball keeps rolling downhill, and that involvement increases with every comment, project, or contribution.

Dos and Don'ts of Motivation

As with any form of coaching, there is a right way and a wrong way to motivate. Leaders often confuse the two. This list should clear up some of that confusion.

Dos

- Listen for passion and interests.
- Create options.
- Show support for learning.
- Help create a vision of success and passion.
- Recognize that people are motivated differently.

Don'ts

- Talk about your expectations.
- Shoot down any ideas.
- Ignore celebrating the small wins.
- Say that progress can't be measured.
- Ignore how people like to tackle a challenge.

Motivating Is Guaranteed to Fail If You

- Do not listen carefully to underlying issues.
- Are manipulative.
- Focus too narrowly on one motivational factor.

Characteristics of Great Motivators

What does it take to be a great motivator? Great motivators

- Create noncynical environments.
- Help to clearly identify passions.
- Think about how to encourage and motivate others.
- Talk about how work can make a difference.
- Know when and how to present a challenge.

Tips for the Motivation Conversation

When it comes time to have your 20-Minute Motivation Conversation, revisit these helpful tips:

- Stay focused on issues that are within the person's control.
- Stay positive but realistic.
- Stay on the bigger picture; show perspective.
- Stay away from false promises.
- Stay on track with what is best for this individual.

Now Try This

Motivation begins with insight into the thinking and priorities of others. Here are a dozen ways to begin a comfortable 20-Minute Motivation Conversation:

1. What kind of work do you find most exciting?
2. What kinds of challenges are most interesting for you?
3. What are the decisions or projects that you would like to be more involved with?
4. What are the ways in which you would like more control or more choices in your work?
5. What are the ways in which you see your work as being appreciated or recognized? How can we improve on this?
6. Of the seven motivation factors that you have identified as most effective, which two or three are must-haves for you? Why? How might we build them into your work?
7. What could we do to make the work more meaningful for you? What else?
8. What are some creative or innovative projects that might be interesting for you?
9. What new learning or new skills would you enjoy developing?
10. What kind of plan could we put together that would help maximize the factors that you find most motivating?
11. What kinds of achievements have been most satisfying for you? How might we enhance your sense of achievement?
12. What is one topic or issue that you'd like to discuss with your manager? This might be one that you just haven't had an opportunity to bring up.

PART 3

THE 20-MINUTE MENTORING CONVERSATION

CHAPTER 7

START WHERE THEY ARE, NOT WHERE YOU ARE

"You never forget your first mentor; I got mine when I was 17 years old, a junior in high school, and practically illiterate. I was in my high school mechanics class at the time—car mechanics was in my blood. I loved cars. I built cars, repaired cars, and raced cars.

"One day my third-period English teacher, Mrs. Whittier, dropped by to see if the class would take on the project of giving her car a new set of brakes and a change of oil. I would have been a natural for the job, but I quickly looked away, knowing that I was failing her class. *The Scarlet Letter* was way beyond my reading ability, not to mention my interest level.

"One day I guess she noticed that I had a hot rod magazine open to some jazzy car photos. She asked, 'Are you reading about that?'

"'Well, not exactly,' was my answer, 'but the pictures are great, and I can usually guess what they are saying. I can read maybe half of it sometimes,' I confessed.

"'The pictures *are* great,' she agreed. 'What if we made that magazine and others like it your reading assignment this year?'

"'You mean instead of *The Scarlet Letter*?' I asked.

"'Well, we'll talk about that later, but for now we set a goal of reading three hot rod magazines—and I'll work with you after school on it.'

"'I can try, but you know, I really don't read much at all.'

"'I know that,' she said. 'Deal?'

"Mrs. Whittier started me with the basics, and within three weeks I was reading my magazines from cover to cover. I guess I knew a little more about reading than I thought; I was really just lacking confidence and interest.

"Well, through the rest of my high school experience, Mrs. Whittier was there for me, advising and teaching—just there. She even helped me get into the local junior college, then advised me into a local university. She eventually retired and moved to Florida, but she taught me valuable lessons in discipline and hard work—and how to believe in myself. I have always sought informal mentors ever since, and I now mentor many people in return."

A local businessman named Jim, who was coaching my son's soccer team, once told me this inspiring story after he heard about what I did for a living. From a kid who couldn't make his way through a hot rod magazine, he's done pretty well for himself: he now owns five muffler franchises in the area and truly gives back to his community.

What got Jim started? How did he switch tracks from failure to success? Someone—in his case, a teacher—saw something in him, took an interest, and took an extra step to bring him along and develop him into something more—more than he ever thought he could be. What Mrs. Whittier did was find Jim in his place (where he was) and start from there.

The task of the leader is to get people from where they are to where they have not been.

—Henry Kissinger

The Right Starting Point Makes All the Difference

Mentorship is a delicate balance between two people at different ends of the experience spectrum. Oftentimes we seek out as mentors those with experiences that we have yet to have or wisdom that we've yet to begin to gain. Where you begin the process makes all the difference. For instance, if Mrs. Whittier had insisted that Jim read beyond his capacity—too far, too soon—she might never have fostered a love for reading in the first place.

Being a good mentor means reading between the lines, knowing how to help the mentee in a way that will be mutually beneficial for both of you. It's probably a new role for you, so it may take some getting used to. So far you've been a leader-coach and, next, a leader-motivator. As you explore your own leadership style, I stress the importance of working as a leader-mentor.

However, a big mistake that leader-mentors make is to try to bring employees to where they are—what they think the employee should be doing—instead of starting where the employee is right now. They mistakenly think that every employee wants to be like them or to develop as they did, so they guide with something in mind, something that just may not be right for the employee.

Where the employee is might not just be his or her skill level—i.e., the employee may not be ready for management or that promotion yet—but also where the employee fits with the organization or even just his or her current job goals. Remember that the best leaders bring out the best in their people, people as unique individuals with specific skill sets, passions, and interests; mentoring should be no different.

Don't see your role as mentor as just another "sleight of hand" way of leading; act like a true mentor and guide the employee from his seat of power, based on what he does best, how he best learns, and so on.

Meet the employee where he is; find common ground and build trust by seeing things from the mentee's perspective. When you use mentoring to create many mini-versions of yourself, this simply creates a gap between leaders and mentored employees. In this case, the 20-Minute Mentoring Conversation becomes just another thing for both the leader and the employee to do—and this takes away the true pleasure and results of a great mentoring experience.

Your people will learn from you and develop at their pace, not yours. So it's important for you to find out where they are in terms of development and where they would like to be—and how you may be able to support them and connect them to what they may need.

Identify Their Passions as a Firm Starting Ground

Let's face it, leadership is full of challenges. You don't need another one! So make mentoring easier on yourself (and your mentee) by engaging in a true partnership of ideas. Take the burden off yourself by opening up the mentorship experience with a discovery of the mentee's passion.

Use this time to find out

- What really inspires him?
- Why did she take the job?
- What does he really want to do?
- What was her last exciting project?
- And why?

While there is a structure to the 20-Minute Mentoring Conversation—as with our two previous conversations—use the structure to your advantage. Mentoring is a different role for most: not quite friend, not quite boss. Use the relaxed nature of the mentor role not only to learn what excites your people, but to get excited yourself.

So often your job as leader takes you away from people—the business of your day, the crushing responsibility of knowing every minute detail about the company's finances and future, and the natural distance between employer and employee. These issues can become barriers after a while, but if you let it, mentoring can be your way back to mutual one-on-one conversations with your people.

And not every conversation has to fit like clockwork into the formula. Sometimes the leader's just sharing some experiences will be enough—a story, a learning experience, an anecdote, or even a parable, shared in a sage, earnest way during a 20-Minute Mentoring Conversation can truly inspire a mentee in ways you could never imagine.

Dorothy Leonard and Walter Swap, in their article on "Deep Smarts" (*Harvard Business Review*, September 2004) talk about learning as an experience; they stress the importance of older or more experienced employees helping younger ones merely by sharing experiences they've had.

"Many times in our lives," say the authors, "both professional and personal—we need either to transfer knowledge we have built up over years of experience from our heads to someone else's (our child, a junior colleague, a peer) or we have the reverse need: to somehow access those bits of wisdom accumulated in someone else's cranium."

Mentoring can be your chance to share your vast experience with employees on a wide range of levels over a wide range of shared passions. Many times, a story can truly help illuminate a key point, much as Jim's story about his mentor, Mrs. Whittier, helped me open a chapter on mentoring. When you're helping people gain new experience on the job, setting it up properly in a 20-Minute Mentoring Conversation and having this kind of one-on-one "debriefing" with an experienced leader can be invaluable.

This kind of development takes a little more patience and is perfectly suited to a structured 20-Minute Conversation. So, help your employees identify their passions, like Jim's hot rod magazines, then, slowly and systematically, help them find *The Scarlet Letter*, as Mrs. Whittier did. Find out where they are first. Conversations like this one can help:

Leader: Linda, I thought we should take a few minutes over a cup of coffee to see how you're enjoying your new job. I'm glad we could make this time.

Linda: Me too. Things seem to be going okay. I'm learning a lot and meeting new people, which is great.

Leader: I know you're on a fast learning curve now, but if we look into the future, what do you want to be learning?

Linda: Well, it's hard to see beyond the next month or so. I can think of a couple of things that might help me now, though.

Leader: I can think of a couple of things, too, like you learning more about the budgeting process.

Linda: Well, budget would be helpful, maybe later in the year. What I could really use now is better negotiating skills.

Leader: Tell me more about that. Why negotiating?

Linda: Well, it seems that every time I need data from another team, they have their own agenda and priorities, and they don't see my needs as very important. I think I need to be more creative in how I deal with them—help them see what's in it for them, you know, negotiate.

Leader: I see what you mean. It makes sense; it's a special skill. I've never been the best negotiator myself, but I do know a great negotiator, Matt in Purchasing. What if I set up a lunch for you with Matt—you could pick his brain for an hour, ask some basic questions, and then you and I can come up with a plan to help you develop your negotiating further.

Linda: That would be great! Anytime next week works for me.

The Three Big Truths of Mentoring

In this example of a give-and-take mentoring conversation, the leader obviously had some ideas as to where Linda's development needed to go, but Linda had a different idea and goals in mind. The leader was fortunate that Linda asserted her need; a more passive employee might have just agreed with her manager, and the mentoring conversation would not have been as honest and useful to either party.

In asserting her need, Linda was honest and open; in hearing her needs and responding with an active solution to help them both, the leader proved himself to be an avid listener. No wonder the conversation went so well: being honest, being open, and being a listener are the *three big truths of mentoring*:

1. *Being honest.* Being a leader does not mean being the right person for every job—or every situation. Suggesting someone who has more expertise than you have in a certain area is not passing the buck, but merely being honest about your strengths and weaknesses and leading your mentee in the right direction. Be honest; admit what you don't know or are uncomfortable teaching or dealing with. What are the limitations to discuss, if any? For example, your employee may have trouble with another manager, and you might feel that it's best for him or her to get advice on dealing with this from someone other than yourself, because you know the other manager on a personal basis. Or perhaps one of your employees is having marital problems, and you don't feel comfortable advising him or her on these matters (or qualified to do so). Is there someone else you could advise the employee to speak with, such as a counseling professional recommended by the company Employee Assistance Program?

2. *Being open.* By being open to discussion, you reveal that you want to hear what is going on and that you are inviting conversations; you want to show your curiosity by asking open-ended questions that don't require multiple-choice answers or limit the response in any

way. Remember, questions that do not have a yes or no answer can often be the most revealing in mentoring conversations (or any conversation, for that matter). Open-ended questions are things that invite an open response, such as "What are your thoughts on . . ." or "How might we go about this?"

3. *Being a listener.* The famed management consultant Peter Drucker once said, "Most communication problems were just misunderstandings in communication." I think most leaders and employees will admit that we don't really understand each other that well, but we want to, and, most of the time, we think that we do. Listening closely and openly can help you check your understanding of what the employee is saying and help you guess at his or her underlying goals, needs, fears, and so on. Witness how the leader in the previous conversation, who obviously wanted to talk about budgeting, listened to Linda's concerns about negotiating with other departments to help funnel the conversation not where he wanted it to go, but where he actively needed it to go. Remember that communication is a road traveled by two people, not just one, and thus the destination should be a compromise of both, not a bending of wills from one to the other. Sure, the leader could have forced the issue back to budgeting, but what good would it have done if Linda's real issue was negotiation?

Cheers hearten a man; but jeers are just as essential, they help maintain his sense of balance.

—Jay House

Skills Can Be Learned:
The Mentoring Conversation

Remember that listening *is* a skill and, like all skills, if you don't possess it naturally (i.e., if you're not a "born listener"), you can acquire the skill of listening over time, with practice. Consider the following discussion to see how listening has a big impact when mentoring:

Employee: I don't think I want this new job.

Leader: What is your concern about the job?

Employee: Well, it sounds like I will need to do a lot of one-on-one interviewing of the senior leadership team, and I've heard that they can be hard to deal with.

Leader: You've dealt with challenging situations before and done well. It sounds like there might be something specific about senior leadership that worries you?

Employee: Well, it's not just interviewing that group that's the problem, but I will need to present my findings back to them in a big team meeting, right?

Leader: So it's not the interaction with senior managers that concerns you; it is the presentation process and the challenges that it might present.

Employee: Yeah. I don't have the strongest presentation skills, and I've heard that senior people can push back pretty hard and really put people on the spot about what they are hearing.

Leader: Sounds like we might set a goal around improving your stand-up skills first; would that help? Maybe copresenting with me for your first time in that team meeting?

This is another great example of the leader as mentor. Hear how she at first explores the issue of her employee's reluctance to interview the senior leadership team. However, through listening and open-ended questioning, she quickly realizes that it's not the interviewing that is the employee's problem but the presentation of the responses from the interviews.

Listening closely, and actively questioning the mentee, can single-handedly turn a conversation from a chore to something miraculous, game-changing, and successful for you both.

Finding Common Ground

Look at the two mentoring conversations we've read thus far; both of them featured "homework" for both the mentor and the mentee. In Linda's case, she got to look forward to a lunch with Matt from Purchasing to help her with her negotiation skills. In the latest conversation, our mentee got assurances that the leader not only would help with presentation skills but would actually be available to copresent the findings for the first session.

Likewise, each of your 20-Minute Mentoring Conversations should have a clear focus and a clear "next step" to work on for the next meeting; it doesn't matter if that meeting is two weeks or a month away.

Meetings without such next steps are incomplete; they might as well not have happened at all. With every 20-Minute Conversation, you're beginning a process, not having an event; there will have to be next steps, small goals, and follow-up if the meeting is to be taken serious by the mentee, or, for that matter, produce results for you, the mentor.

Remember, the idea of these meetings is not merely for you to get to know your employees better, act engaged, or indulge yourself in the corporate consultant "flavor of the month" sundae; it is to create exactly the type of action plans and results that we've seen thus far in this chapter.

Some of the Push-Pull behaviors that will be most helpful to you in conducting 20-Minute Mentoring Conversations are these: *questioning*, *finding common ground*, *visioning*, and, of course, *listening*. Let's look at an important behavior that is very underused in most mentoring conversations: finding common ground.

Finding sincere common ground during this conversation will help you establish trust and credibility with your employee. Remember, people trust others whom they believe they have something in common with and who they feel can understand their situation and their thinking and feelings about a certain issue (or issues).

Many leaders think that talking about the weekend sports scores or, if addressing a female employee, the latest Oscar nominees means finding "common ground." That may help a bit, but there is more. Finding common ground must be done in a sincere and honest way. Here some examples of common ground language you might use to get you started:

- "We both have some concerns about this project, but maybe for different reasons."
- "Let's look at what we can do together. For instance, we can set some small goals that we both feel good about."
- "No one wants to feel like they are not appreciated for what they do. I certainly don't, and it sounds like you don't, either."

It is important that you find your common ground wherever you can, even in the simplest things, such as, "We both want to be successful and build our reputations in this company; let's see what we can do together to work that out."

Seeking common ground will help every leader be identified as someone who has values, thoughts, and experiences that are close to those of others in the group; it will be a bridge toward creating a relationship and understanding with *each member of the leader's team*.

Mentors need to get in sync with their employees and teams if they are to be seen as one of them, i.e., they need to send the message that "we have common goals and concerns" or "we are together in wanting success for you, the employee, and the team as a whole."

What's more, these goals need to be sincere and have weight, and they *must* be backed up by action plans, as we've seen in both of the mentoring conversations we've studied so far in this chapter.

Recent research in leadership success by S. Alexander Haslam, Stephen D. Reicher, and Michael J. Platow, presented in their forthcoming book, *The New Psychology of Leadership* (Psychology Press, 2009), shows the power of understanding the values and opinions of followers, and then finding consensus. The book "advances the argument that leadership is a group process grounded in the creation, management and control of group identity—a shared sense of 'us.'"

To create this "group identity," it is first necessary to find shared experiences, interests, passions, and principles. So by having this 20-Minute Mentoring Conversation, leaders and employees can discover that they are on the same page and find common ground in how to move forward with an action plan to accomplish before the next meeting.

Unfortunately, this isn't common practice for either leaders or employees. Too many managers have told me that they just "didn't click" with an employee. When I asked why or what they did to remedy the situation, all they could tell me was how different they were from their mentee; they simply could not find the common ground.

But when I hear such blanket statements, I have to ask myself how hard that manager or leader looked for the common ground. We can't work only with the people we click with; as part of a team with a group identity, we must all recognize the fact that we bring different abilities, personalities, interests, and even temperaments to the table.

Remember that you hired so-and-so for his or her specific valuable traits as a team player. Every team needs a mixture of dreamers, doers, planners, and creators. If you are a visionary and you "click" only with visionaries and thus hire only visionaries, who will do? Who will draw up the blueprints or facilitate the meetings or manufacture the prototype or fetch the coffee or make sure that you have enough brochures printed for the seminar?

Finding common ground isn't just about making life easier in the workplace; it's about connecting with each member of the team on a personal level, despite their temperament or personality. Abraham Lincoln once said, "I don't like that man; I need to get to know him better."

"What have you done lately to get to know your employee better?"

I ask this very question of managers whenever they claim that they don't click with an employee. "You didn't click?" I ask. "Well, maybe it's not them. What have you done lately to get to know this employee better?" Their answers are typically that they "did not do enough," but why? Because they did not know how to get to know the employee better.

Now I Want to Mentor You

"Now I want to mentor you" is probably not the right way to lead into your 20-Minute Conversation! Why? Because it sounds huge and scary to people. Here is what people think of, immediately, when you say, "Now I want to mentor you":

- "What does this mean?"
- "What's going to happen to me?"
- "What am I supposed to do?"
- "Why me?!?"

These are some of the more unpleasant thoughts employees have told me would run through their minds if their manager announced, "Now, I want to mentor you."

Instead of freaking your people out, try phrases like

- "Let's spend some time talking about your future development."
- "Let's talk about what you see for yourself in the future."
- "Let's talk about your career development."

Part of getting ready for an informal meeting will be your own understanding of what you're comfortable teaching—and advising—about. You'll also want to be prepared to "hand off" a mentee to a more appropriate party, like Matt from Purchasing in our earlier example, who might be better suited to share in the mentoring responsibilities.

Now Try This

The following quick checklist will help you to better understand what you can teach and when you might connect the employee to someone else who would make a better mentor for a specific skill.

First, as the mentor, check off five items on this list that you would be willing to teach or that you feel you can help your employee learn. Next, check off five items for which you might be able to connect your employee to someone else who can help him or her learn, and lastly, circle three of these items for your own development. For instance, which of these would you like an informal mentor to guide, advise, and teach you about?

1. Presenting to upper management
2. Setting work priorities and career goals
3. Using a problem-solving methodology
4. Managing time
5. Working with technical systems
6. Working with teams
7. Working with budgets
8. Using negotiation skills
9. Motivating myself and others
10. Making clear decisions
11. Managing projects
12. Managing change
13. Communicating, both written and oral

14. Solving conflicts
15. Giving and receiving feedback
16. Handling customer relationships
17. Planning strategically
18. Handling work stress effectively
19. Running an effective meeting
20. Being creative and innovative
21. Being persuasive and influential

CHAPTER **8**

YOU'VE GOT A STORY— YOUR LIFE

Attorney Len Tillem is also a radio talk show host here in the San Francisco Bay area. I often listen to his show as I'm driving the crowded freeways, and obviously I'm not alone. Every day Len starts his conversation with his listeners by inviting them to call the station "with their stories."

And call they do; they have endless stories to tell and questions to ask. It's always riveting to listen to. After all, they're not just giving us—and Len, the show's expert host—their various legal problems, they're telling their stories. To his credit, the radio host always finds a way to glean a learning point for his listeners. Maybe because every story has a point, it also always has a purpose.

Stories tap into the way we think; they connect us, teach us, and validate our life experiences. Everyone has a story, because every one of us has had life experiences that have taught us valuable lessons. Best of all, it does not matter if the stories are about our failures or our successes; if they are crafted well and told well, they have a lasting and meaningful impact on people. So, given the importance and effectiveness of storytelling, let's take a moment and consider your mentoring stories: how to develop them, tell them, and learn from them.

Perfection Is Overrated (and Undereffective)

It was the fall meeting of our local training society, which met quarterly at a popular hotel in downtown Los Angeles. My workshop time was 10 a.m., and I was just starting my presentation to 40 HR training professionals.

I had prepared hard for this presentation, down to the last detail, since this was my first opportunity to present in front of my peer group. Did I mention that it was very early in my career as a consultant? I knew my lines, I knew my key concepts, and I knew the questions my audience would be asking me. In fact, I thought I knew it all!

But despite my endless hours of preparation, an ideal starting time (not too early, not too late), and the intimacy of sharing the room with a small audience of my peers, they were not impressed. In fact, at the time they seemed to me the toughest, most unfriendly group of people I had ever encountered.

They did not laugh at my jokes, brushed off my fancy slides, and seemed indifferent to everything I had to say. I found myself retreating from the group—literally backing up as I talked, looking for some room and putting some distance between us. I was thinking to myself, "Well, this is a first. It's the last time I'll try to present to *this* organization."

As I was retreating, I bumped into the training table at the front of the room, where I kept my notes, a half-finished cup of coffee, and water. "Maybe I'll just sit on the table," I thought, "make it look like I'm relaxed."

However, as I backed into the table seat, I did not realize that what was under the white tablecloth was not an ordinary table, but just a temporary aluminum picnic table, the kind that folds up in the middle. (I was told later that the hotel had run out of regular tables.)

You guessed it; I chose to rest my butt right in the middle of the table. The two of us came down with a crash—the table and I crumbled together, with water and coffee flying, and I wound up on the floor, stunned and humbled.

The room was silent until everyone realized that I was okay—just embarrassed—then the folks in the audience erupted into laughter. They thought this was the funniest thing they had seen in a presentation. As we settled down, they began to tell about their most embarrassing moments (one told about a pigeon flying around one presentation full of people, dropping poop on people's heads), and on and on it went, one story after another.

Eventually I realized that this was what they had wanted all along—not a presenter who was perfect and knew everything, someone who was well rehearsed and was reading his speech off of cue cards, but someone human, just like them, who makes mistakes, sometimes looks ridiculous, can make fun of himself, but is definitely *not perfect*.

"I don't have to be the perfect presenter," I thought to myself that day, and this realization completely changed my mindset; you might say it revolutionized it, and gave me the freedom to be myself and enjoy the experience of communicating with others. (Thank goodness it came at the beginning of my career as a consultant!) From that day forward, I was a changed professional, one who had learned to laugh at himself and find the joy in his work. In short, I had found my story.

And the best part was, it was a story that lent itself to so many situations, a story about my failure, my experience, and my learning. Over the years, I've told this story many times to trainers and consultants whom I've been fortunate to mentor—who might have been taking themselves and their content too seriously—and I could always say, with perfect authority, "You don't need to be perfect."

I would still be a qualified and, some might argue, effective consultant without my clumsy antics oh-so-long ago, but I wouldn't be the same. That experience, that story, taught me not just the gift of imperfection, but also the gift of loving what you do and not taking it quite so seriously.

Stories are a special means of communication, a way to connect with people and your employees like no other. As a means of communicating effectively, they are second to none; they have an impact on people at an emotional level and have a clear learning point. They connect at a rational level also.

The Seven Gifts of Storytelling

Your stories will generally be pulled right from your life experiences. They don't need to be about the biggest thing that has ever happened to you or a way to drop the names of all the special people you've ever met. They can be about something small but significant—mistakes and successes, both professional and personal. They just need to contain an insight or learning, something that taught you a lesson—a turning point in your thinking.

Stories are so great because, if you think about it, they are something you do (or "tell") all day long. If you're the guy in the break room regaling everyone with your weekend antics, you can be a great mentor-slash-storyteller. If you're the gal making all her girlfriends spit out their coffee while you're spilling about your latest blind date, you too can be a great mentor-slash-storyteller.

We're all storytellers; stories come naturally and easily to us, and we slip into them so often because they're the most effective way of communicating a message. Stories are the universal language; we all understand them.

Stories allow you to connect on a personal level, building both trust and understanding with your employee in the process. Your willingness to disclose a vulnerable experience, how you came through it, and what you learned from it becomes a sign that your employee may do the same.

Using stories as a mentoring tool helps you as a leader to

1. *Connect with the way your employees feel and think.* Storytelling helps us share emotions rather than impart them. When I clumsily fell in front of that group of local HR training professionals, I learned that people get engaged when they have the opportunity to share. When you

see storytelling as a back-and-forth process, you invite a stronger connection between mentor and mentee.

2. *Show empathy with a pressing situation through your own experiences and reactions.* Leaders are often seen as distant people on pedestals. Storytelling makes you more empathetic and human as you relate your own experiences, which, despite the barrier that exists between employer and employee, are often quite similar in nature to theirs.

3. *Take learning to a new, deeper level of understanding.* When we see a graph or chart, we may take it in and be impressed by the statistics (or even intimidated by them). When a story is used to impart that same information, the understanding of it increases tenfold.

4. *Be more inspirational and down-to-earth without being preachy.* Sometimes your mentees need more than mere information; they require inspiration. Stories transcend the typical "locker room pep talk" to become something that is much more meaningful and down-to-earth.

5. *Help employees think about issues and the future by examining an experience from the past.* We learn from history, whether it be national, local, or commercial. When you tell your employees about the mistakes made by the characters in your story, people like "Bob" or "Jane" or "Mary" or Frank," they can learn from those mistakes and avoid them rather than repeat them.

6. *Engage at a nonthreatening emotional level.* Even if your story is a cautionary tale or a warning to your mentee,

the verbal tone of storytelling is such that your words are less threatening by their very nature.

7. *Help employees gain more encouragement and explore new possibilities.* Much of a leader's work is communicated through e-mails, memos, intermediaries, and third parties. When you are engaging with someone one-on-one, you afford him the hope that his voice will actually be heard.

Follow These Four Rules for Developing Your Stories

Why are stories so important? For one thing, they span all styles of learning; for another, they bridge all socioeconomic, cultural, and educational backgrounds. I've watched many a gifted storyteller wow diverse crowds with complex physical and cultural makeups simply by speaking in the universal language of storytelling. Chances are you have too: at church, in politics, at community events or business luncheons.

I've also seen otherwise gifted speakers struggle with challenging, sophisticated information by presenting it in a straightforward, linear, story-free way. I've often sat in crowded auditoriums or intimate seminars, watched the eyes of the audience members glaze over, and thought, "If this guy would just cap this off with a simple story, we'd all understand it a little better."

Think of the last time you presented a bunch of factual material to a group, a department, or an individual. Chances are that you got a lot of blank stares until you related the information you'd just presented in the form of a story; then the lights went on, the eyes opened, and the heads started nodding.

Why is this the case? According to Doug Stevenson, the author of *Doug Stevenson's Story Theater Method*, stories are effective because they bridge all learning styles:

1. *They get people information in a visual way, helping to create a picture in others' minds.* Some people simply have to "see" something to truly appreciate it. That's why you have readers and moviegoers, newspaper subscribers and TV watchers.

2. *They are auditory, hearing lessons that people can process.* The way auditory learners come to understanding is almost primal; you can trace it back to the way stories were handed down from generation to generation.

3. *They are kinesthetic, transferring how one feels and is affected emotionally into an authentic experience that one can take away.* Kinesthetic learners gain understanding from movement, and even the most sedate storytellers get animated when they are sharing a learned experience.

The Four Quick Rules for Creating Your Story

Good storytelling doesn't just happen. Even the most "natural"-seeming speakers are often well versed in telling their stories, having told them multiple times to multiple audiences. I myself have learned to be a better storyteller rather than coming to it naturally.

When you have an ally in a great personal story, it's a shame to waste it because you don't feel comfortable sharing it or don't know how to pull it off. Everyone can be a storyteller; we do it a hundred times a day. It's only when you're put on the spot and forced to tell a story in a business setting that it might get intimidating.

As I said earlier, if you can regale your buddies with a great story by the water cooler on Monday morning or have your girlfriends wiping their eyes after you share the details of another horrid blind date, you can master the art of storytelling.

These four tips will help.

1. *Set up.* When a novelist starts a mystery, he doesn't go straight to the crime; he sets the mood, letting readers know what the gloomy mansion looks like or what town the creepy killer lives in. Likewise, setting up your own anecdote helps communicate "why" you are telling your story. Where did it happen? When did it happen? Was it last year, last month, or this morning on the way to work? Some details about the context of the story are necessary for understanding. What were you thinking or doing? Letting people know the basics—where the story took place, what time of day it was or how recently, and what it meant to you—will go a long way toward grabbing their interest quickly.

2. *Who and what.* Next, share the "characters" in your story, i.e., the people who were involved. In my experience, the fewer parties that are involved in a short mentor story, the better. For instance, was it just you, or is this a third-

party experience? Was this something that happened to your old boss from three companies ago, or did it happen to Robert in Accounting? Then discuss what the problems, conflicts, or issues are that will need to be overcome in the story.

3. *Resolve it.* A story without an ending is like a meeting that never happened; what was the point? Was it resolved well or not? What did you have to do to resolve the issue? Did you have to use new strength or call on something that you've used before? Did you get help? From whom and how?

4. *Lesson learned.* The ending, or at least the solution, to your story is how it was resolved. What you learned from it and, by association, what you want your mentee to learn from it is the lesson that you are trying to share. So, what is the point you're making? What did you learn, and what do you want to remember? How did this experience change things or create new awareness?

Brooke and Elyse: Models of Mentoring

Storytelling can sound esoteric and oblique in theory, but let's see how it can be used for practical purposes in sharing experiences to make a mentee see a solution for herself. In this storytelling example, Elyse, the group leader, is having a conversation with Brooke, her project leader, about Brooke's frustrations in her dealings with Craig, a manager of a team that Brooke needs to have support her project:

Brooke: He just seems to push all my buttons in every meeting; his attitude doesn't seem helpful at all.

Elyse: How have you handled that? What have you talked about with Craig?

Brooke: Well, I'm so frustrated that I walk into the meeting already angry and loaded for bear. I can hardly think straight, let alone address what's going on. Plus, I'm under a lot of pressure to meet the project deadlines, and the project's scope keeps changing daily!

Elyse: You know, Brooke, I had a situation last week where I was ready to explode at the slightest thing—but it wasn't at work, it was at the local bagel shop. I'd had a bad start to the day. First, my alarm didn't go off on time, then the car decided it needed to stall three times on my way to get coffee and a bagel. So, I'm in the bagel shop, and just below the surface I'm steaming, almost itching for an argument, for some reason. I'm like a ticking bomb that's ready to go off, and I'm thinking about this guy ahead of me who's taking forever, it seems, to give an order. "Make up your mind already," I'm thinking. He finally orders everything you can possibly fit on a bagel. "This guy could really stand to lose a couple of pounds; I can't believe what he's ordering," I confess to thinking. Now I'm looking at my watch and tapping my foot nervously; I couldn't possibly be more frustrated, when suddenly the guy's paying for his order and says to the counter girl, "I want to pay for this lady's order, too, to thank her for waiting for me to make my decision." I'm stunned! I tell him, "You don't have to do that." "I know," he says, "but sometimes I just like to commit a random act of generosity—pass it on if you feel like it." Brooke, I have to tell you, it blew me away. I mean, it really took the wind right out of my sails and totally changed the way I felt about the day, my mindset, and humankind in general.

Brooke: Yeah, I can totally identify with your feelings going into that bagel shop—it's like I'm itching for a fight when I go into the meeting with Craig.

Elyse: Sometimes you've got to just know that you're in a state of frustration and not let it take over how you see the world or, in this case, Craig's team. Sometimes you have to choose to 'commit a random act of generosity.' Take a deep breath and choose a positive mindset."

A wise man will make more opportunities than he finds.

—Francis Bacon

Less Is More: How Short Stories Can Solve Big Problems

In the previous story, Elyse could simply have responded to Brooke's frustrations by saying, "You need an attitude adjustment." But that message sounds a little blunt without any precursor or cushion, so instead she sat back, considered her own attitude-changing adjustment, and told a brief, entertaining, universal, and pointed story. What's more, she admitted having certain basic human faults to allow Brooke to let her guard down; Elyse confessed to being impatient ("Make up your mind already!"), rude (tapping her foot), and even ungenerous of spirit (suggesting that the guy in front of her could afford to lose some weight).

Through very basic storytelling skills, Elyse took Brooke out of her unpleasant situation with Craig and focused her attention on this very simple story; in no time at all, Elyse had gotten to her ultimate point: "Sometimes you have to choose to 'commit a random act of generosity.' Take a deep breath and choose a positive mindset."

True, she could have gone straight there, and perhaps Brooke might even have considered it. But now Brooke has done something even better; she's internalized it. Now whenever Craig upsets her, Brooke at least has a frame of reference, a place to go where she's not alone, where even her boss has had to deal with this kind of situation, and now she can truly have that "attitude adjustment" without resenting Elyse for not taking her quite seriously enough.

As Elyse's anecdote shows, your stories can be short and to the point; they can also come from any life experience that applies to the situation. Don't feel that you're limited to telling only workplace stories. However, whether it comes from the bagel shop or the corner office, your story simply has to have a beginning, a middle, and an end, and, most importantly, a point.

If you're struggling or reaching for some fresh material, some possible stories might include

- A time you needed to deal with a difficult person
- A failure and how you came back from it
- A success against odds that seemed impossible
- A bad feeling you had that you ignored or paid attention to
- Seeing someone who made a mistake and how he or she handled it
- Any conflict and how you approached it, resolved it, or learned from it
- A conflict and how you handled it successfully
- A bad decision and what you learned from it
- A crossroads in your career and your choice
- Losing your passion and how you regained it
- A mentor you had in the past and what he or she taught you
- How to deal with organizational politics

> Vision is the art of seeing things invisible.
>
> —Jonathan Swift

The Bricklayer and the Visionary

"I'm working like a dog," I told my boss, "at least ten hours a day, six days a week. I hardly have time to look up, I'm so buried in the details of this project. I think I've lost my way. I know it won't last forever, but I think I've forgotten why I'm doing all this."

"You need a vision," my boss told me. "You know, the big picture. Why does all this count?"

"Yeah, I guess so, but what exactly is a vision?" I asked.

In reply, he told me this well-known story that (I feel) bears repeating here: well, imagine that you're exploring a new town, just walking around, and you come across a construction site where three bricklayers are working, and you ask the first workman, "What are you doing?"

"Well, I'm earning $12 an hour laying these bricks."

Then you ask the second bricklayer, "What are you doing?"

"Well, I'm building a wall."

And you ask the third bricklayer, "What are you doing?"

"I'm building a cathedral for the glory of mankind!"

My boss looked at me and asked, "What are you doing? Are you just laying bricks, or are you doing something bigger?"

"Suddenly, I got it. What I was doing was changing the way this company would do business from now on."

When a client recently shared this story with me, it confirmed my notion that storytelling really is one of the easiest ways of imparting both wisdom and inspiration to a troubled mentee.

Now Try This

Identify one story from your life, something that changed the way you see things forever. You can take this story, whatever it is, and use it as a template for *any* story that you share with a mentee. Simply follow these questions to create a storytelling template of your own:

1. *Give the story a title or label.* (For instance, my story might be called "The Picnic Table Incident"!)

    _____

    _____

2. *Why is it a good story to tell?*

    _____

    _____

3. *What happened?*

    _____

    _____

4. *What are the learning points for you or one of your employees?*

_____

_____

CHAPTER 9

WHEN TO USE THE 20-MINUTE MENTORING CONVERSATION

"Dale has been doing the same job for 3½ years. At first," his boss admits, "it was a tough learning curve; there were lots of new people to meet, plenty of industry lingo to get down, and his share of stiff deadlines to meet, but now he can do it just by rolling out of bed. He is definitely comfortable—not that there's anything wrong with being comfortable in your work, but I think he is ready for something new. I think Dale would agree, if only I could 'get him to see the light,' so to speak. I think he believes that being comfortable at work is more advantageous than I do.

"Dale seems really good with customers, handling problems pleasantly and dutifully staying in touch when it's called for. Right now, most of his work is done in the back of the house on the operations side, with little customer contact unless he is called in specifically to solve a particular problem.

"I've hinted to Dale that it might be a good idea for him to get out into the field more; it would entail a little more travel than he's used to right now, but I think it would be really good for him. Here is someone who could move up one day, not just stand still. Unfortunately, he just doesn't seem to hear any of my hints. Alan, I think it's time to do a 20- Minute Mentoring Conversation, but I'm just a little frustrated. I mean, how do I start?"

Dale's boss is right on in her analysis of Dale; comfortable doesn't always equal peak employee performance. Instead of sleepwalking in the back, he needs to get out to the front of the store more often and do what he apparently does so well: interact with customers and solve problems on the front lines.

It's not that he isn't performing in the back of the house, but when you can do your job in your sleep, it's time to wake up! Is Dale comfortable? Probably, and, as I said, comfortable doesn't equal bad. But has he reached a plateau? Maybe, and plateaus aren't always the best place to be to foster employee success. And Dale's boss is right about something else as well: the 20-Minute Mentoring Conversation would be an effective way to find out for sure.

When is it the right time for *you* to use a 20-Minute Mentoring Conversation? Use a 20-Minute Mentoring Conversation in situations that involve

1. *Advancement.* An employee is asking questions about her career or wants to explore other opportunities within the company.

2. *Potential.* You see undiscovered or underappreciated skills and talent, or you believe that the employee needs to stretch into more learning.

3. *Prevention.* You are concerned that the individual might be making mistakes in his career decisions.

4. *Networking.* The employee needs to expand her network of contacts within the company in order to develop to her full potential.

5. *Retention.* You want to make sure that an employee is retained in the company for the long term, and, what's more, that the employee actually sees a future for himself in the company.

Mentoring: A Three-Step Plan for Success

The language and behaviors used in mentoring are going to be primarily focused on Pull behaviors. If we look at our three steps to mentoring success, they might be something like this.

Step 1: Identify

The first step is to clarify what this conversation is about. We can do that more effectively when we

- *Statement of purpose.* Such as, "I'd like to talk with you about your development.
- *Ask open questions.* For instance, "What aspects of your present job make you feel more comfortable? What have

you been considering for future development?" These types of questions encourage the person to actively participate.

- *Find common ground.* You can present clear evidence of understanding when you find common ground with your employee. For instance, you might say, "We both know that continuous learning is a great way to keep your skills fresh," or something like, "And we have a hard time finding the time to learn a new system, but my team needed me 24/7 to keep doing my old job. Here's what I did . . ."

Step 2: Involve

We really need to be clear about what potential learning or perspective would be helpful to this person.

- *Ask focused questions.* We can help the employee focus on the issue at hand when we ask questions like, "Tell me more about your interest in leadership roles," or, "It sounds to me like you're most interested in getting a higher profile for yourself in the company, and being a leader is one way to do that."
- *Summarize.* Summarizing allows us to bring clarity to the conversation. "So you're thinking about a project leader position in about a year or so?" Here we can feed back to the employee what we think he or she has said. Not only is this an opportunity to summarize, but if we haven't heard correctly or if the employee has been

unclear, we can get this straightened out and avoid losing precious time.

Step 3: Initiate

It is important to identify the ways in which we can connect for development. We can do this more effectively when we help the employee to initiate some plan of action:

- *Vision.* What is your vision for how the employee can best fit into the organization? How can he or she act, specifically, to produce more results? Don't keep this information to yourself; use the mentoring conversation as an opportunity to share your vision with the employee. "Here's what I can see us doing together," is one way of initiating a mentor-mentee action plan. Or, "Let's create a picture of where you could be in a year."
- *Suggest.* Suggestions are a great way to offer clarity and decisive action when it becomes appropriate during the conversation. "My suggestion to you is this: why don't we begin training Kara to take over your job now? That way we can free up 20 percent of your time now for something new."
- *Offer an incentive.* Sometimes mentees need help to get the process started or, for that matter, to feel comfortable starting the process at all. Offering an incentive helps give them a reason to begin. "What I would be willing to do is talk with Kara to make sure she is on

board with this. I'll make sure that someone can cover her spot on the team. What I need from you is a list of what you could train her on now."

Remember that this is not just idle talk; every conversation needs a purpose going in. Likewise, that purpose doesn't always remain static. In fact, it may change as a result of information that you discover during the conversation. However, as the leader, you will be focused and clear in identifying a possible development goal.

The smallest of actions is always better than the noblest of intentions.

—Author Unknown

Mentoring Learning Activities

When a conversation leads to action, it becomes doubly effective. Here are some authentic ways in which you can introduce learning activities before, during, after, or in concert with your 20-Minute Mentoring Conversation(s):

- *Job shadowing.* Ask your partner to attend or take part in a work meeting or activity with you, and compare your observations afterward.
- *Job modeling.* Bring your partner to an activity or a meeting where he or she can observe and learn a key skill from you. Be sure to debrief the person afterward.

- *Joint meeting.* Introduce your partner to your contacts and your "network"; encourage the participant to meet with others and learn from their experience and viewpoints.
- *Lessons of experience.* Introduce your partner to other senior leaders. Invite one of them to lunch with the participant, or arrange a meeting time. Ask about the person's hard-won lessons of experience, how she's managed her career, and her views on current company trends and projects.
- *"Oddball" thinker.* Encourage your partner to spend some time with someone in your organization who has an interesting, thought-provoking, or atypical view about an important topic. Be sure to debrief the person afterward.
- *Problem-solving discussions.* Engage in focused sessions to resolve difficult problems or situations.

The Mentoring Conversation in Action

What might a representative mentoring conversation sound like? What might it look like? How can a simple conversation that takes less than half an hour lead to specific, concrete results that will have an actual effect on an employee's productivity and effectiveness at work?

Let's see, shall we? Remember Dale, who was so comfortable at work that he could practically do his job in his sleep? Here are some ways in which Dale's boss might "wake him up" with an effective, but brief, 20-Minute Mentoring Conversation:

Boss: Dale, I'm happy that we can spend 20 minutes or so to talk about your job and some future possibilities for you here at work. What are you experiencing with your current work? Are you comfortable?

Dale: Yeah, things are going well. I've got a good handle on things. I mean, even with the changes from corporate, I think I'm still under control.

Boss: I think so, too. If we were to expand your opportunities to have an impact on the business, what would you be interested in learning or doing?

Dale: Well, I am feeling pretty good right now, and I haven't really thought about doing anything different.

Boss: I can understand that. One thing I've noticed is that you're very good at working directly with the customers when you need to do so.

Dale: Helping customers is always fun and interesting; I learn things from them that help with our new products. But it takes time, and it requires being on the road, which takes me away from home and my new son.

Boss: So it sounds like you enjoy working directly with clients; it's just the time spent traveling that presents a problem for you, especially with your new child?

Dale: Yeah; too bad the customers can't come here.

Boss: That would be convenient, and you know there are a couple of times a year when clients are in one place— the quarterly conferences we participate in.

Dale: I've heard about those. I wouldn't mind attending one of them.

Boss: What if we could arrange for you to help with the planning of our display booth, and then perhaps put in a day or two to help man the booth? This quarter it will be held in the southern part of the state. Would that be a problem?

Dale: I'd like to run it by my wife first, but I like the idea of just a couple days away from my work station, and it will give us time to plan my being gone.

Clearly, Dale's boss has her work cut out for her! Dale seems to be a tad more than comfortable at work, and he obviously has home issues—a new son and his wife's desire that he stay closer to home—going against her plans to have him out in the field more often.

But notice how she takes the lead in nudging him ever so slightly out the home office door. Her suggestion that he attend a conference closer to home makes sense for Dale and is a willing compromise to meet him (more than) halfway. Whether or not this will ultimately be effective is up to Dale, of course, and that's the whole point; as mentors—as leaders, really—we can do only so much.

Ultimately, of course, it will always be up to the employee to heed our advice, take our counsel, and welcome (or ignore) the opportunity that is being given to him or her in this conversation. Mentoring is not a way to fix all problems or heal all wounds; none of these conversation models are designed to do that, in and of themselves.

What they *are* designed to do is to foster greater communication at work. Use the 20-Minute Model as a tool to get to the heart of each problem and try to begin working together to solve them, one by one.

In Dale's case, his boss has floated a reasonable idea that will shake up his routine and increase his effectiveness on the job. After that, she can take more and regular steps to broaden his reach, and he can decide whether or not to act on those suggestions. At some point, Dale may resist his boss's ideas, and when that happens, she will know where he stands and his limits on the job.

Does this make Dale a less effective employee or his boss a less effective leader? No on both counts; Dale is perfectly suited to what he is doing now, and furthermore, his boss will know where he stands and can make future promotional decisions based on her best efforts and his comfort zone. At least she now has that information at hand, something that she might not have had without this simple 20-Minute Conversation.

Characteristics of Great Mentors

You will soon find your own mentoring rhythm: what works best for you, what doesn't work at all, and what works "in a pinch" if all else fails. Mentoring conversations, like those associated with coaching and motivating, will soon become second nature to you. Over the course of your first few conversations, it will become important for you to find your rhythm and locate your own specific strengths and weaknesses.

For instance, are you a born storyteller? Can you think on your feet? Or do you need a little more rehearsal time?

Listening to where your employee is feeling the most insecure or unstable on the job will help you craft the kind of mentorship you will need if you are to assist him or her. Remember, who you are at your core will affect the kind of mentor you'll be when it counts the most. While every mentor is different, I have identified several helpful characteristics that all good mentors share:

- They are curious.
- They ask many open-ended questions.
- They promote a trusting relationship.
- They disclose their own mistakes.
- They are devoted to the learning process.
- They know when they are no longer needed.

> When this circuit learns your job, what are you going to do?
>
> —Marshall McLuhan

Tips for Mentoring Conversation(s)

I hope you've seen by now that each of these three types of conversations has its own unique style and flavor, and the 20-Minute Mentoring Conversation is no different. Since this conversation, in particular, relies more on your storytelling, anecdotal, or mentoring talents, you will want to run this particular game a tad differently from the way you might have run your coaching or motivating conversations. Here are some mentoring-specific tips that I think you'll find it helpful to follow as you decide:

- Stay focused on development issues.
- Stay focused on long-term development; encourage the person (e.g., Dale) to stretch his or her comfort zone.
- Stay available; be willing to spend some time connecting with the person around what he or she is learning.
- Avoid one-size-fits-all thinking; recognize individual uniqueness and accentuate it through personalization.
- Stay focused on what the person is learning, not just on what he or she is achieving—rigorously debrief the person's learning successes as well as the stumbles.

Mentoring Dos and Don'ts

Every mentor has his or her own style; please don't think of these sections and subsections as strict scripts or templates to use instead of your own personal style. I am merely providing guidelines for your first few mentoring conversations so that, once the "training wheels" come off, you have your own template in place that is just right for you.

That having been said, there are some general dos and don'ts that I've discovered over the years that I think you'll find helpful as you move forward through the process.

Dos

- Listen for rapport and common ground.
- Invite dialogue.
- Ask questions.
- Learn from the person.
- Create a climate of acceptance.

Don'ts

- Preach.
- Overteach.
- Become judgmental.
- Push at resistance.
- Forget to listen.

Now Try This: Relationship Building Blocks

The success of mentoring ultimately relies on the joint expectations, camaraderie, and commitment forged between you and your participant. The following questions are called "relationship building blocks" because answering them gives others insight into you.

You and your participant might want to talk about one or two of these issues at each meeting. To identify which issues are most personal to you, circle two or three of these questions to help you get ready for this conversation.

1. What is an experience, observation, or lesson learned that has shaped my approach to my life, my purpose, my work, or my family?
2. What legacy might I like to leave?
3. What losses or hardships have I endured, and what wisdom have I gleaned from these?
4. What has surprised me most about my career history?
5. Who is someone that I greatly admire, or who has shaped my life?
6. What burning issues or ideas drive my life?
7. What did your partner learn from the feedback opportunities, and how can it be applied to his or her career development?
8. What was one of my greatest triumphs?
9. Who made the biggest difference in my life during the last year?

Planning the Mentoring Conversation

Now it's time to do some specific planning. Who needs a mentoring conversation? You do, and your employees do. How will you begin? Use our simple three-step process as a guide to help you plan for these specific conversations with your people.

- *Step 1: Identify.* Ask yourself, what is this conversation about? Be specific; this is an opportunity for you to really listen and determine for yourself what, exactly, your employee needs mentoring from you in.

_____

- *Step 2: Involve.* What questions will you be asking? What experiences might you share?

_____

- *Step 3: Initiate.* What ideas do you have in mind for the other person? What suggestions might you make?

_____

CHAPTER 10

WHAT IF
NOTHING WORKS?

About eight years ago, a story appeared in *People* magazine about a brain surgeon practicing in Houston, Texas. While brain surgeons are already noteworthy, this was one extra-noteworthy brain surgeon! His gripping story recounts how he did a third more surgeries than any other brain surgeon at the hospital where he worked, and how his success ratio was 20 percent higher than that of any other surgeon.

Asked how he was able to do all this, he told the reporter from *People*, "Well, most surgical teams prepare extensively before the operation—in detail as to what they will do and how they will do it; they have a good plan on how the surgery will go. What we do is the same, a detailed plan for success. However, we take it a step further: we plan for what will go wrong—we identify the 3 likeliest points at which we might run into trouble and we have a detailed plan how to handle each. So, when we hit a problem we don't need to decide what to do, we just act! And, that makes all the difference."

Well, your 20-Minute Conversations aren't exactly brain surgery, but at times they might seem a whole lot harder. After all, if you just spend six years of study in medical school and pass your exams, you, too, could call yourself a brain surgeon! But dealing with the human psyche in all its complexity still confounds the most seasoned leader.

> In preparing for battle I have always found that plans are useless, but planning is indispensable.
>
> —Dwight David Eisenhower

We have learned much during our time together, but as all leaders know, knowledge is only half of the equation for success. The human psyche in all its shapes, forms, and dysfunctions will continue to confound and challenge us, no matter how proficient we become with these three types of 20-Minute Conversations.

This chapter examines the disturbing, but inevitable, question that we must all ask ourselves at some point: "What if nothing works?" We all know employees who are too challenging to salvage, too problematic to "rescue," and too resistant to direction to ever really coach.

How did they get hired in the first place—or, for that matter, how did they get far enough to come up on our radar screen as being in need of a more serious 20-Minute Conversation? The answers to such questions are many and are often found far downriver from the problems that are affecting us today. The bad news is that these people are now our problem; the good news is that learning to deal with such problems quickly and effectively will solve not only today's issues, but tomorrow's as well.

Our goal now is to end on an upbeat note, even with the challenges of problematic employees facing us. We started this book to craft true top performers with these brief but intense 20-Minute Conversations. This chapter will help us identify troublesome conversations with problematic employees and work to rehabilitate or eradicate these employees sooner so that in fact we have more time for top performers, not less.

Trouble in River City: Three Typical Forms of Resistance

Resistance, disagreement, obstinacy, and other forms of potential conflict might happen in any of the three types of conversations we've explored and prepared for in this book. However, I have found that the greatest potential for conflict comes in the coaching conversation. Why? Maybe because it highlights performance, which we now know can lead to tough consequences if it is not addressed in a truly positive manner.

We have identified three typical forms of resistance that might appear in any of the conversations—and, again, that are most likely to show themselves in during coaching. Here they are:

1. *Denial.* "I did *not* do that!" "It wasn't me!" "I disagree; that's just not true." Sound familiar? Then you're dealing with a serious case of denial. This form of disagreement stems from the defensive place that most of us go to when we're confronted with something that we have been, as we see it, unfairly accused of. Other versions of denial include such comments as, "We see things differently," or, "I don't see why this is a problem." In this case, the employee must be made to see that his or her actions or failures to act are indeed causing a disruption in performance. Your role is to step back from the emotional aspect of the conversation and provide clear, concise "proof" that the team member's denial is misplaced.

2. *Blamer.* "It's not my fault!" "Amy never gives me what I want on these; talk to her." This is like the Teflon defense—nothing seems to stick. The individual takes no responsibility; it's all the other people's fault or another group's fault or the organization's fault. This technique may be better known as finger-pointing or scapegoating, but the results are the same: by blaming someone else, the employee is seeking to elude his or her own responsibility. In this case, it's very important that your people be able to see that even if they are not entirely at fault, they need to take at least partial responsibility, and need to take their part in the action to correct the performance.

3. *Fogger.* In some ways this is a very tough one to spot, as well as to fix. As expectations and feedback are made

clear to the individual, a fog or cloud seems to descend from the heavens over the individual's head. (Trust me; you probably already know what look I'm talking about!) With a cloudy look on his or her face, the person might say, "What are you talking about?" or, "I don't understand what you're saying," or even, "What exactly do you mean?" And, of course, the manager feels obligated to repeat the same message in various ways—again meeting with the same perplexed look of bewilderment. Here the individual needs to understand that your reality will prevail—and that something new must be done. Hiding out in the clouds of his or her own disbelief or denial will neither work nor be tolerated.

Resistance Is Futile! Managing the Three-Step Response to Resistance

There's a line made famous by the most recent incarnation of TV's long-running (and oft-quoted) *Star Trek* series that says, "Resistance is futile!" In many ways, this might be our own mantra for success.

While not all decisions can be handled quickly, or effectively, with a pink slip (or even the threat thereof), regardless of our style of leadership, if we are to breed top performers, we must have the attitude that, in fact, resistance *is* futile.

As the leader who is ultimately responsible for the management, success, and results of this 20-Minute Conversation, you need to be clear about what you will do to handle things when they don't go as planned. Too many otherwise decisive leaders allow conflict to grow and flourish because it is easier to threaten than to act.

Clarity and consistency are the twin pillars of effectiveness when it comes to acting on your resolution to handle resistance. We suggest this simple Three-Step Response to handle these possible disruptions to successful results and performance:

- *Step 1: Identify it.* The first step in dealing with resistance is simply to spot it, bring it out into the open, and stop denying it. Like a referee throwing a flag upon witnessing a foul at a football game, you're simply saying, "Something is not right here, and I see it." Variations of this statement include, "I'm feeling like you're doubting what I'm saying or seeing," or, "You don't see that there is a problem, and I'm concerned about that," or even, "It seems like you deny or disagree with everything I'm pointing out." These are strong, declarative statements that are hard to deny. If any employee hears any one of them, he or she knows that the jig is up. What you are really doing is identifying the problem to begin the process.

- *Step 2: Question it.* By letting the employee know that you are aware of the resistance tactic (denial, blamer, or fogger), you're giving him or her an opportunity to choose another response. This is perfectly reasonable and a great intermediate step before things get out of hand. After all, at times the person might not even realize that he or she has fallen into a defensive place; this can often happen automatically as a defense mechanism from the past. But we don't want to go there; psychologist, mother, friend, father-confessor—these are not our roles. For now, we just want to deal with the present and get a positive result. "What is questioning my feedback going to do for us?" you might ask. Or, "What if the senior VP and the rest of the team see this as a problem?" Or even, "I look bad as a manager when you don't do this. Now can you see why it's a problem?"

- *Step 3: Address it.* After identifying the behavior and openly questioning it, next you must explain the implications of continuing the same actions and encourage a more productive way to resolve the issues. And if things really bog down, move away temporarily—give the employee some space to think about things, then reengage with a short conversation about the issue, perhaps even an hour or a day later. "I need to let you know the downside consequences if we don't work out a plan for this issue," you might begin. Or, "How do you want to handle it from here?" "What is a first step we can agree to?" "How can we do this differently?" "Why don't you think about my feedback, and let's have another short meeting today after 4 p.m. Maybe we can come up with a goal?"

And, of Course, You Might Be Wrong

Harold, a senior new project launch manager, related this story to me at a recent workshop. "I get to work early," he began.

"I've got so much to do right now: calls to Europe, meetings, planning, not a minute to take a deep breath. I pass by Pam's cube, a new supervisor who runs my Asia products division, and I notice that every morning around 8 a.m., she is sitting at her desk reading the newspaper. Now, I've already been at the office since 6:30, and I'm running full blast! How does she have time to read a newspaper? I haven't read a newspaper since last November! I'd better have a conversation with her about this; it just doesn't send the right message—what do her people think when they see her with the paper spread out all over her desk?"

My suggested conversation between the hard-charging Harold and paper-reading Pam went something like this:

Harold: Pam, I wanted to touch on a situation I've been observing and see if we can make some changes.

Pam: Sure. What's up?

Harold: I notice that first thing in the morning, you're spending quite a bit of time reading the newspaper, and I am concerned that people see this and get the wrong message about how you spend your time.

Pam: Well, I really feel it's important to stay up on what's going on. I'm reading the *Wall Street Journal*, and there is always a relevant story about what's going on with our competitors in China. As you know, we need to stay on top of that. And I encourage everyone on my team to do that.

Harold: Oh, I didn't know that.

Pam: Yeah, actually, last week we picked up information that allowed us to make a critical change in our strategy—it will save us a bundle next quarter.

Harold: Oh . . . OK. Well, I'm glad we had a chance to discuss this—maybe you could do a brief 5 to 10 minutes at our next team meeting on what you're doing, what you're finding, and how it helps.

Pam: Sure, Harold; love to.

So, we can see that not everything we see and evaluate is what we suspect it to be—we can be wrong, and a good leader checks out his or her perspective before running wild with it. Notice the phrasing that Harold used to deflect his own high emotions about the matter and zero in on something specific: "Here is what I'm seeing, and here is what it's leading me to believe."

"Am I wrong?" he seems to be saying. "I certainly could be." Far from weakening your position or sounding unleader-like, these are truly delightful words that anyone would want to hear.

A Special Breed: Generation Why?

Gen Y—or, as these people are commonly referred to by leaders all around the country, Generation Why???—is really quite a challenge. At 76 million strong, Gen Y has become a force to be reckoned with and has quickly asserted its personality in the workplace. What drives, motivates, and rewards Generation Y?

According to *Time* magazine, "Friendship is such a strong motivator for them that Gen Y workers will choose a job just to be with their friends." And flexibility, technology, and connectedness are equally important: "It feels normal for Gen Y employees to check in by BlackBerry all weekend," reports *Time*, "as long as they have flexibility during the week."

Consider a story related to me by the chief financial officer of a Fortune 100 company recently. At a new employee meeting, the CFO finished up his remarks as quickly and efficiently as possible, but still the 50 new hires in the room, mostly Gen-Yers, were obviously restless. This group had a really short attention span, and many had their laptops and their BlackBerries open and their fingers twitching—multitasking, or whatever.

"I took a walk around the room," this HR VP related to me, "just to check on what these folks were into—and my worst fear was realized: it wasn't e-mail to constantly stay in touch with new business issues that they were looking at; it was Facebook and shopping that were dominating the computer screens I was scanning."

"What are these people thinking?" the CFO asked me as soon as his presentation was over. "I'm trying to introduce them to the business, and most of them are off in la-la land! Somebody needs to teach these folks basic business etiquette."

Welcome to Gen Y—those born between 1977 and 1998, some 76 million of them. By all accounts, they are the future of corporate America. With boomers retiring or, more recently, being phased out into early retirement to make way for the younger, less costly employees and Gen X workers who are taking their place, Gen Y has become the new go-to population for new hires around the globe. And, I told the skeptical CFO, they were not being deliberately rude during his presentation. In fact, as a group, I have discovered that they are rather polite; they just have other priorities, and at times they are a bit too casual about the work-play gap.

According to the Boston Consulting Group, adapting to an aging workforce and shifting needs to incoming Gen Y employees was rated the challenge whose importance will grow the most in the future. And according to CSI Millennial Study 2008, 72 percent of Millennials (Gen Y) express doubt that their managers know what is important to them about work, while 34 percent report being "unenthusiastic" about their work.

Who are these Gen-Yers, and why are they so challenging? Generally speaking, here is what they care about:

- Directness over subtlety
- Action over observations
- Teamwork over individual tasks
- Flexibility over rigidity
- Constant learning over the status quo
- And, feedback, feedback, feedback!

Applying the Principles of the 20-Minute Conversation to Your Gen Y Employees: A Checklist

I've seen firsthand the frustrations that my peers—and perhaps yours as well—feel when dealing with their Gen Y employees. It can often feel as if you're speaking an entirely different language. But consider the cautionary tale of Harold and Pam; first impressions can be deceiving.

If you'll recall, Harold was running around thinking that Pam was lagging behind when, in fact, she was merely doing on-the-job research. Before writing off the members of Gen Y as too fun-loving, casual, or socially-oriented, consider their strengths as well and go on a case-by-case basis. Don't just lump all your Gen Y employees together. Chances are that some of your Gen Y hires will be too casual for you, but not all. Getting tunnel vision or stereotyping this valuable—and huge!—segment of the workforce will cost only you, not them.

The implications for coaching, motivating, and mentoring this very specific and personal population require a new mindset for leaders; but you don't have to reinvent the wheel. Through personal observation, anecdotal evidence, and plenty of research, I have created a checklist that will get you started in applying the principles of the 20-Minute Conversation to your Gen Y employees:

- Let them know clearly and directly how what they are doing affects the world.

- Show them that this job gives them an opportunity to grow and learn.
- Ask them what they are curious about.
- Show them a future with the team or the company—spell it out!
- When possible, give them some flexibility and a sense of freedom.
- Challenge them and let them multitask when needed.
- Let them have opportunities to be social and connect with others.
- Give them some structure and process.
- Teach them the etiquette of the organizational culture.
- Give them the truth and lots of feedback during all three conversations.
- Get them goals quickly—multiple career options, and some future plans.
- If possible, make the latest technology available to them—they want the leading edge and the "cool" factor.

Some managers report to me that their Gen Y employees are always asking, "How am I doing?" One manager told me that they ask him this question, "Like every day; at first they seemed like high maintenance, but once they understood how to perform, they became my best workers." Yes, they sometimes require lots of attention; they are used to it And they are your future success as a team and as a company, so plan your 20 minutes well, and they will soon be your top performers.

Top Performers in Turmoil: Your Toolbox for Turbulent Times

As I write these final words of this final chapter, the American economy is teetering from recession to depression and back again almost daily. I can't help but notice how it's affecting not only my own consultancy business, but also those businesses for which I continue to consult. Now more than ever, it would seem, good people are falling on bad times.

It may be that your department is shrinking in size; it may be that your hiring pool has grown exponentially even while your hiring needs are dwindling by the day. It may mean shifting the wrong person into the right job and right back out again if he or she can't seem to perform at pace.

As belts tighten at home and at work, you may find yourself using these 20-Minute Conversations more and more often, either to encourage employees or to deal with resistance. Whichever is the case, I have tried my best to equip you with the tools you'll need to face any leadership challenge and craft true top performers regardless of the economic climate—all in 20 minutes or less.

In my work, through my clients and through countless seminars, questionnaires, and responses, I have identified not just *how* these 20-Minute Conversations work, but *why* they are so effective in the modern workplace. By now you have no doubt seen how to personalize a strategy for each conversation and for each employee. As you memorize and familiarize yourself with the format of each conversation, you will quickly adapt to using what works for each particular situation.

We have explored the unique and valuable attributes of why and how coaching works, what employees get from motivation, and when mentoring is the most appropriate strategy for you to take. We have covered countless listening skills, and through reading and practice, hopefully you now feel comfortable not just with each of the three types of conversations, but with the value of the conversations themselves.

In addition to the worksheets, tips, strategies, and tactics I've provided within each chapter, the appendix to this book contains additional valuable and timely advice for nearly any question you may have or problem you may encounter as you warm to the idea of these 20-Minute Conversations and, what's more, begin to implement them more and more often as part of your ongoing growth and maturity as a top-performing leader of top performers.

YOUR 20-MINUTE LEADERSHIP TOOLBOX

From time to time, we hit those inevitable plateaus at work. Things are going okay, but they could be going better. We've gotten comfortable with our 20-Minute Conversations, but maybe a little too comfortable. For those days when you just need an extra tool from your leadership toolbox, I have provided some additional worksheets, checklists, tips, and tactics to address specific issues as they arise:

Leaders, Heal Thyself

We've all heard the story of the shoemaker's children who have no shoes. And this is an important point, and one that I stress with all the managers that I train: it's almost unfair to ask managers to have 20-Minute Conversations with their employees when they themselves are not getting them.

Everyone needs the opportunity to be a top performer. If you are not getting the conversations that you need from your management, then you might be running on empty. To find out, ask yourself the following series of questions:

- How do you make sure that you're clear on performance targets?
- Are you getting the feedback and clear expectations that you need if you are to be at your best as a performer?
- How do you keep yourself fully engaged when you need a new challenge or more motivation and interest in your work?
- Are you getting the advice and support concerning your career goals that you're looking for through informal mentoring conversations?

Check off one or two 20-Minute Conversations for yourself from the following topics, then be proactive with your boss in getting a dialogue going, so that you are taking responsibility for your own successful performance:

Coaching

- Help identify problem issues and new creative options.
- Get more direct feedback and ideas on how to succeed.
- Share more expertise and experience in order to perform current tasks better.

Motivating/Engagement

- Find more learning opportunities.
- Help make the work meaningful and understand personal definitions of success.
- Share more information that would help make work more satisfying.

Mentoring

- Be a connector to resources, people, and other parts of the organization.
- Focus more on the big picture and promote deep thinking about careers and the company's future.
- Share advice and insight about how to achieve personal success.

Successful Feedback Skills

When we spoke earlier about feedback, I stressed how important it was. To elaborate on that discussion, here is a series of the most successful feedback skills I've identified over the years.

Skill 1: Be Descriptive, Not Evaluative

Provide a description of what you have observed—a specific behavior or task. If you give feedback that is evaluative, you increase the chances for defensiveness because of the broad nature of that feedback.

- *Example:* "I really want more information on future needs in your group. Your presentation deals more with past performance; let's concentrate on the next 18 months."

Skill 2: Be Very Specific

You want the receiver of your feedback to improve specific skills, tasks, or behaviors that are observable and measurable. If the feedback is general in nature, it provides little help in improving performance.

- *Example:* "You did a great job on your presentation. Your overheads were simple and direct, and you allowed people to get involved with thought-provoking questions."

Skill 3: Comment on Behaviors

Feedback on behavior is much easier for people to hear and change. Examples can be given that have been observed and that have direct impact on performance. On the other hand, feedback that concentrates on the person is too general and sets up a situation in which corrective action is limited.

- *Example:* "By coming to the meeting late, you give others the impression that the meeting is not important to you."

Open-Ended Questions and Coaching

These are questions that cannot be answered with a yes or no. They add a lot of value to the coaching process by

- Showing the employee that you are sincerely interested in hearing what he or she has to say.
- Inviting participation and an open exchange of ideas, opinions, and explanations.
- Making employees more comfortable. People have a tendency to feel more in control when they are speaking.
- Providing an opportunity to learn more about the employees' thinking and feelings.
- Helping to gain commitment and uncover potential pitfalls.

Examples

- "How do you feel about . . .?"
- "What are some examples of . . .?"
- "What do you think about . . .?"
- "What is your point of view about . . .?"

Following Up on a Coaching Conversation

In order to give ongoing feedback to the employee on his or her success or on new changes that may be needed, the coach should be active in the follow-up process. The feedback should be based on the coach's observations and should be recorded or documented.

Observe the Behavior

- Have behaviors changed?
- What opportunities are there for positive reinforcement?

Problem-Solve

- Revisit priorities and goals.
- Does the work need to be replanned?

Stay Positive and Future-Focused

- Look for small improvements.
- Use positive feedback to encourage continuous improvement.

Document Observations and Changes

- Record successes and changes.
- When, where, what, and how has this made a difference in performance?

Coaching Agreement

Make a copy of the joint agreement for both parties:

Conversation Date	Action Steps	Completion Date	Notes

1. _____

_____

_____

2. _____

_____

_____

3. _____

_____

_____

4. _____

_____

_____

5. _____

_____

_____

_____

Getting Results: Why Employees Don't Get the Job Done

Lack Skill: They Don't Know How

- Lack of instruction, orientation, or training
- Improper feedback or lack of feedback

Lack of Tools and Processes: Something or Someone Keeps Them from It

- Material or system restrictions
- Not enough time
- Wrong supplies, materials, procedure, or process

Lack of Willingness: They Don't Want To

- Previous good work unrecognized
- Burnout
- Unhappy with manager or job
- Lack of motivation

Stretch Assignments

Developmental assignments have been shown to be one of the most effective methods of learning. The "stretch assignment," as it is known, may be small in scope with limited responsibility or larger with key responsibility. These assignments are usually work-related, but on occasion may be completed in an employee's community. All developmental assignments need to be well structured and completely debriefed to ensure a good, useful learning experience.

Following this three-step process, suggested by the Center for Creative Leadership, is a great way to present structure to the stretch assignment and help ensure success:

- *Step 1: Specific observation.* Set up an opportunity for the employees to observe an area expert completing a specific task. It should be something that the employee has identified as an area of development or interest.
- *Step 2: Limited responsibility.* Identify a limited role or task that can be completed in a short amount of time. This gives the employee an opportunity to experience what a given project or the acquisition of a new skill would entail.
- *Step 3: Complete responsibility.* Here the employee takes over a task or responsibility. He or she is fully accountable for the success of the activity. The employee in some cases may elect to stop at the end of any one of the steps along the way, depending on the learning assessment.

A full debriefing of each step is important, so that key learning points are discussed and explored. Some debriefing questions are:

- What new ideas did this observation give you?
- What's changed for you as a result of this observation?

- What was most interesting for you during this experience?
- Were you comfortable?
- What is there about this experience that you would want to repeat?
- What has been your best learning from this experience?
- How would you change the way you approached this assignment?

Getting to Know You: More Relationship Building Bock Questions

The success of mentoring ultimately relies on the joint expectations, camaraderie, and commitment forged between you and your participant. The following questions are called "relationship building blocks" because answering them gives others insight into you. You and your participant might want to talk about one or two of these issues at each meeting:

- What is an experience, observation, or lesson learned that has shaped my approach to my life, my purpose, my work, or my family?
- What legacy might I like to leave?
- What losses or hardships have I endured, and what wisdom have I gleaned from these?
- Who is someone that I greatly admire, or who has shaped my life?

- What burning issues or ideas drive my life?
- What did your partner learn from the feedback opportunities, and how can this be applied to his or her career development?
- What was one of my greatest triumphs?
- Who made the biggest difference in my life during the last year?
- What's the biggest risk that I've taken, what were the results, and what did I learn about myself from it?
- What advice would I like to give myself? Why?
- What are the sources of joy in my life?
- How would my best friend describe me? Why?
- What's the smartest decision I ever made and why?
- What has been my biggest failure or disappointment in my career?
- What have I learned from the coaches and mentors in my life?

INDEX

ABOUT THE AUTHOR

Alan Vengel is the founder of Vengel Consulting Group, Inc. He is the author of *The Influence Edge: How to Persuade Others to Help You Achieve Your Goals* (Berrett-Koehler Publishers, 2001), and coauthor of *Sprout! Everything I Need to Know about Sales I Learned from My Garden* (Berrett-Koehler Publishers, 2004)—two bestselling books on leadership, management, and negotiation.

Over the last 25 years as a consultant and speaker, Alan has presented seminars, programs, and keynotes to more than 500 corporations. When they want their employees to become powerhouses of influence, industry leaders such as Cisco, Disney, General Electric, Kraft Foods, and Microsoft hire Alan.

Alan is located in California and travels frequently across the country to bring his unique vision for 20-Minute Conversations to leaders of companies both large and small. He has a wide network of trainers and consultants globally, including offices in Paris, Shanghai and Hong Kong.

Alan has developed the award-winning training programs "The Influence Edge: Getting Work Done without Authority"; "3 Leadership Conversations: Coaching, Motivating, and Mentoring"; and "The Negotiation Focus: How to Negotiate Win/Win Agreements." He also represents the best in career development products through Career Systems International. Vengel Consulting Group workshops create real business learning using practical, easy-to-use skill development tools for immediate application by all workshop participants.

His interactive Webinars help organizations leverage learning throughout the company and his leading edge online tools are practical and easy for participants to use on the job.

You can learn more about Alan at his Web site, www. vengelconsulting.com. While you are there, you can read excerpts from all three of his current books; join a mailing list to be frequently updated about Alan's new projects, tips, and tools; and peruse past articles on leadership, management, influence, and negotiation.

Also, as you visit Alan's Web site, you can take a short version of the Vengel Motivation–Engagement survey to learn how to keep yourself engaged.

For immediate information on training and the 20-Minutes to a Top Performer Webinar, please e-mail Alan directly at alan@vengelconsulting.com or call 925-837-0148.